A WARTIME MEMORIES (

With my Best wishes.

Colin Russell

A WARTIME
SCHOOLBOY:
Memories of Fradley

COLIN RUSSELL

ISBN: 978-1-901253-59-7

First published March 2020

Cover illustration: Patricia Kelsall

Design and layout by Anne Loader Publications
Published by Léonie Press
13 Vale Road, Hartford
Northwich, Cheshire CW8 1PL
Great Britain
Tel: 01606 75660
email: anne@leoniepress.com
websites: www.leoniepress.com
www.greenridgespress.co.uk

Printed by Poplar Services Printers Ltd,
Poplar House, Jackson Street, St Helens WA9 3AP

Myself, aged eight, in 1942

Author's note

I HAVE written these memories of my school days for two reasons. Firstly for my own pleasure of reliving the early years of my life, a lot of it spent in the company of good friends, in the Staffordshire village of Fradley – which changed considerably over the wartime years. And secondly for any one else who may be interested enough to read them.

I dedicate this book to my mother and father, who managed to feed and clothe me during a difficult time for all parents, to my friends who lived in Fradley during the wartime years and also to the teachers of the three schools who encouraged me to learn.

Colin Russell
December 2004
(Introduction to original privately
circulated typescript)

Contents

Illustrations

A WARTIME SCHOOLBOY: MEMORIES OF FRADLEY

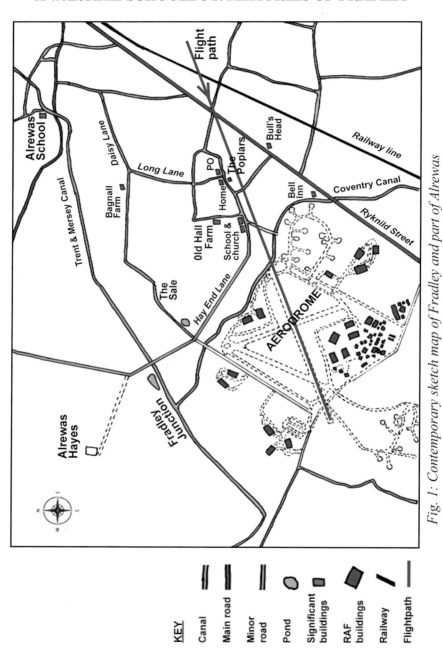

Fig. 1: Contemporary sketch map of Fradley and part of Alrewas

KEY

Canal	
Main road	
Minor road	
Pond	
Significant buildings	
RAF buildings	
Railway	
Flightpath	

St Stephen's School
Fradley
1938 - 1942

Chapter 1

EVERY MORNING, before reaching school age, I walked with my friends, who were all older than me, as far the school gate and waved them goodbye. I always felt it un-fair that they should be allowed into school when I was left to wander home alone, so I made a couple of attempts to get myself admitted before I was old enough.

On the first occasion, I waited at the gate for half an

Fig 2: Fradley School

hour or so after the other children had gone into school. The teacher happened to look out of the window, saw me and assumed that I was my friend John Hardy, who was away from school owing to illness. At a distance, we looked alike, both of us having blonde hair. The teacher came outside, hoping to confront the pupil whom she thought was playing truant. I ran away, thinking that she was coming to tell me off, which got my friend into trouble when he returned to school.

I managed to actually get into the school on the second attempt. One Monday morning, my friends took me into school with them and told the teacher that I was now four and a half years old and would like to start school. She told me to sit in one of the desks and the lesson started. About an hour later, there was a knock on the school door. The teacher opened the door and from the conversation that ensued, I recognized the sound of my mother's voice.

An agreement was apparently reached without my mother entering the room, that I should remain in class until lunch time, avoiding what my mother knew was a strong possibility that I would disrupt the whole class, if I was to be dragged out of the room, kicking and screaming. As most of my friends went home for lunch, it was easier to let me walk home with them and then lock me in the house to prevent me returning.

It was a lonely time for me during term time. I often roamed, alone, through the fields surrounding The Poplars Farm, opposite to where I lived. The Watson family never objected to the village children, whatever their age, using the fields as a meeting place to play games.

When only four years old, I enjoyed running around amongst the cows and horses, much to my mother's fear that one day I would be trampled to death. She was pleased when I reached the age to be within the control of the teacher in the classroom.

Looking back over some of the events during my young childhood, I cheated death several times. Even when very young, I played in the field opposite our house in which, in addition to the horses and cows, there was a small fowl pen with a removable top. My friend John and I were encouraged to get inside it by an older boy, who replaced the top, trapping us inside. He then dropped in a lighted match which set the straw alight.

Fortunately we were small enough to escape through the opening where the hens entered. After waking up the family during the night, when having a bad dream about the events of the previous day, I was questioned by my mother about the burn marks on my hands and told not to go into the field again. I think the ban lasted only for a short time and the fright did not deter me from lighting fires myself whenever I could. Often I managed to set light to a bit of dry grass on the vegetable garden, explaining to my mother that I had done it with the help of the sun through an old magnifying glass when she knew very well that I had, somehow, stolen a match from the kitchen and struck it on a stone.

In the corner of the kitchen at 'The Mount', where we lived, was a brick-built boiler, where water could be heated for washing. The clothes were placed into what was known as the copper, which held about ten gallons of water, filled by bucket from either the tap or an external water bosh of soft rainwater and heated by a fire below it. It seemed to boil away all morning, belching out clouds of steam through the open door.

It was the pride of every housewife to ensure that the washing, when hung out on the clothes line to dry, looked exceptionally white. There was a small block in a muslin sleeve called a "blue bag" which was put into the water at some stage which actually whitened the washing. I never did understand how that worked. I think a lot of the women secretly inspected the washing on other people's lines to see if it was as white as their own. It seemed to me that if the washing looked good, they were also thought of as clean-living.

When not in use, the copper had a wooden cover placed on top and mother always hung newspaper down the front in an attempt to disguise the fire hole. One morning whilst my mum was upstairs dressing my younger sister, I managed to reach the box of matches which had been left on top of the boiler, struck one and set light to the newspaper which hung down the front. The flames flew up in front of my face, luckily missing my skin, but singeing the front of my hair.

I shouted "The kitchen is on fire!", and ran outside before mother could catch me. She was too preoccupied for a while, putting out the fire, to chastise me but ensured that I served my punishment later in the day.

I was very pleased, when legally I was allowed to commence my education at St Stephen's School, Fradley, in 1938. After my earlier escapades, I needed no introduction to the teacher, Miss Dobson, affectionately known by the pupils as "Dobby Hoss". She accepted me this time, as I was accompanied by my mother.

So at last, Colin Russell was now able to start his education, much to the satisfaction of not only myself but also my mum, who now definitely knew where I was, for at least most of the day.

There were only about twenty pupils at that time, their ages ranging from four to eight years old. On reaching the age of eight we moved on to Alrewas School.

Miss Dobson was a Victorian lady, about fifty years old, who had long hair plaited and wound round into two buns, one over each ear. She lived at Rolleston on Dove, just north of Burton on Trent, and travelled to and from Fradley each day, by train from Burton to Alrewas and on a bicycle

Fig. 3: In the corn field before the war with Mrs. Jones, Mrs.
Woolley, my sister Joyce and my mother

from her home to the station in Burton and again by bicycle from Alrewas to Fradley School.

Occasionally during the winter months, especially when there had been a deep fall of snow, she would be late arriving, but I don't ever remember her being absent for a whole day. Always, during the afternoon, she set work for us to do the following morning, in case the train was late arriving. The subject was usually arithmetic, thinking that would keep us well occupied.

The school was always opened up early each morning by the cleaning lady, Mrs. Olive Harvey. The single large classroom was furnished with children's desks, a teacher's desk, a blackboard on an easel and a couple of storage cupboards. A kitchen containing a sink with a cold water tap was attached at the rear and a cloak room, with a couple of rows of hat and coat hooks, formed the entrance porch.

Just inside the entrance door to the classroom, the attendance board hung on the wall. It listed the five weekdays with columns for the number of pupils attending both morning and afternoon classes.

A door at the rear of the classroom led out into an enclosed yard where the toilets were situated, each of them discharging into a hole in the ground. The smell was something that we got used to after a few weeks of starting school. The boys' urinal didn't have a roof, so during the winter there appeared some interesting patterns made by the boys who used the loo after a good fall of snow.

The only heating was by two coke-burning stoves in the classroom, which were lit by the cleaner and were usually red hot by nine o'clock. Unfortunately they did not heat all of the room, so during the winter our desks were arranged in a semi-circle around them to at least keep our legs warm.

A few of us always arrived there about half an hour early, in order that we could ask Olive to help us with our maths, before Miss Dobson arrived. When the school door was opened, a strong smell of polish was always noticed firstly, followed, in winter time, by sulphur from the coke burning in the stoves.

Our teacher could not understand how I could always get the answers to my sums correct during the early morning exercise, when she was not there and yet failed to do so if she set similar examples later in the day.

On the odd occasion that Miss Dobson decided upon punishment for someone who misbehaved, she would push up one of our shirt sleeves and give us a smack across the arm. It felt a bit sharp, so I thought that I had devised a way of avoiding it by removing the buttons from my shirt sleeves and asked my mother to sew up the cuffs.

The next time the teacher tried to push up my sleeve to expose my arm, it wouldn't move, but before I could rejoice, she gave me a sharp clout across the back of my bare leg. At that time boys wore short trousers and stockings until they were about eleven years old or even older if they were not very tall.

Most mornings were spent on arithmetic and particular importance was made of learning multiplication tables from two to twelve. Each table was printed on to a coloured card, approximately 12 inches (300mm.) wide by 24 inches (600mm.) high.

We walked individually, or sometimes in couples, around the playground, reciting a table out loud, until we had learned it "parrot fashion". When we were confident that we knew it, we would go inside school and ask to be tested. If we could recite it correctly to the teacher without hesitation, we were allowed to commence learning the next higher table. By the time we had completed all of the tables up to twelve, we were able to answer any multiplication question fired at us.

Handwriting was practised every day, concentrating on one letter at a time. We had to write several lines repeating the same letter until Miss Dobson was satisfied that we had formed the correct shape. We were then encouraged to write short essays, using the words we had learned.

Several afternoons each week were spent on art and crafts. In addition to drawing and painting, I learned to knit, make woollen pom-poms, weave small baskets and the like with raffia and form patterns with coloured paper. There was also a box of wooden blocks of various sizes with which we used to build all sorts of objects.

Most days we would listen to a story and afterwards would be questioned on the contents, to ensure that we had been listening. Owing to the differing ages of pupils in the school, reading lessons were given in small groups and Miss Dobson called each child individually up to her desk to check their progress.

A WARTIME SCHOOLBOY: MEMORIES OF FRADLEY

A music lesson was given each week, with the teacher playing the piano accompanied by several pupils playing instruments forming what was loosely called 'the band'. The favourite instrument for the boys was the drum, whilst the girls were usually given tambourines or the triangle. Fortunately the school was a good distance away from the nearest house, so I am sure the noise didn't disturb anyone.

Every morning during a break from lessons, the teacher made a large jug of Horlicks and each pupil was given a small mug of it to drink, together with an arrowroot biscuit to eat. It was usual for us to draw a face on the biscuit with our pencil, until one day Miss Dobson spotted one covered with black lead and stopped the practice for a while.

Those of us who lived near to the school walked home for lunch unless there was a deep snow fall, when we would all take sandwiches, which was probably as well, as we would have played in the snow rather than going home.

Periodically the schools inspector, affectionately known by the children as "Daddy Reynolds", arrived on his motorbike.

He usually sat near to our teacher in deep discussion. Although I did not ever hear what was said, he obviously asked questions about each one of us, by the way he looked at us individually. I was called out to the front of the class by him, to ask me why I had not attended school one afternoon.

Mother had decided one lunch time that I needed my hair cut, so instead of returning to school, she took me to Lichfield by bus to the barbers. It had obviously been noted on the register that I had been absent, so after leaving the school, Mr. Reynolds went immediately to see Mum and warned her that if it happened again, she would get into trouble.

After Daddy Reynolds retired, a Mr. Craddock, who drove a car, used to visit the school. He looked even more severe, so no one risked having time off, unless we were ill.

Chapter 2

BY THE TIME war was declared on Germany on 3rd September 1939, work on the construction of the nearby aerodrome had already started. There was very little security to begin with, except for a few Army personnel in trenches and they were more interested in whether an attack was going to come from the sky, rather than being concerned about a few children wandering around. So in the early stages, with some of my friends, I walked along the country lanes, across the airfield, in wonderment at what was happening. We were later prevented from inspecting progress, when large rolls of barbed wire were stretched around the perimeter, gates incorporated on entrance roads and concrete pillboxes, to protect the guards, constructed at prominent positions along the canal side.

On the Sunday morning, when the announcement was made that Britain was at war with Germany, for the first time in my life, I saw my mother cry. Although we didn't have a wireless, the news quickly spread around our little village. She had witnessed the First World War, when her brother fought in France, and had more idea of what to expect than the younger people in the village.

Some of our own fathers were instructed to work on building hangars and administrative buildings, until they were called into the forces themselves.

Fig. 4: Aircraft hangar built near to the canal at Fradley

Fig. 5: Pillbox built on the perimeter of the airfield at Fradley

My father was a bricklayer by trade, so he was involved from the early stages.

Royal Air Force personnel started to arrive almost immediately, a lot of them being billeted in the village until accommodation on the airfield was built for them. An RAF officer, accompanied by the local policeman, called at each house to check the number of bedrooms and assess how many airmen could be accommodated.

Fradley village was a very small community in the 1930s. There were only thirty-five to forty houses, although there were as many as ten farms and a few small holdings. In the centre of the village was the shop and post office, owned by the Hardy family, which, particularly during wartime, was a lifeline for the villagers.

Although it was necessary to do some shopping in Lichfield, most food and essential items were stocked in the shop.

Identification cards and ration books were issued to everyone, each carrying the personal identity number of the holder. The area code for Fradley was OTLN and each family was given a number – ours being 65 – and each member of the family their individual number, depending upon your status.

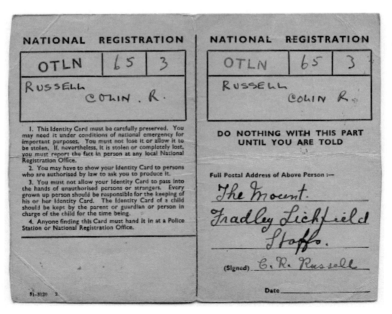

Fig 6: My identity card

The senior member, usually the father, was given number 1, the mother number 2 and so on down through the children, the eldest child being number 3. My identity number was OTLN 65 3. As I was so young when it was issued, my mother signed my name on the card.

To buy groceries, which were all rationed, it was necessary to be registered with a grocer. The villagers who lived in Fradley were obviously registered with Mr. Hardy, who removed the coupons from each ration book at the time when the weekly allocation was collected from the shop.

The weekly ration for each person was as follows:-

Bacon and ham	*4oz. or 112 grams*
Sugar	*8oz. or 225 grams*
Butter	*2oz. or 56 grams*
Cooking fats	*8oz. or 225 grams*
Tea	*2oz. or 56 grams*
Cheese	*1oz. or 28 grams*
Jam	*2oz. or 56 grams*
Sweets	*2oz. or 56 grams*

Coupons had to be used for other rationed foods, such as biscuits and tinned food, if it was available. Sixteen coupons per week were allowed for these things but when it is realised that a small tin of fish took all of the sixteen coupons, no one over-ate.

Most of the villagers registered with Percy Coates the butcher in Alrewas for their meat ration. He had a van, usually driven by Tom Durose, who delivered the meat to the surrounding villages. Meat was rationed by price and the allowance for one person was a shilling's worth (5p).

Clothing coupons were also issued, so these needed to be saved until there were enough to buy a new pair of shoes or a shirt. As I grew out of mine so quickly, my mother could not afford to waste coupons on buying new clothes for me, so whenever possible, she would buy second-hand things.

I was fortunate that a relative of my dad, who lived in Canada and had a boy older than me, occasionally posted

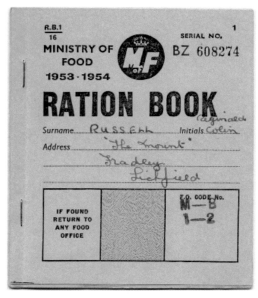

Fig. 7: Ration book

a jacket or a pair of trousers on to me.

Petrol was also strictly rationed and was allocated only to those businesses who required transport. Anyone who was fortunate to own a car purely for social use, was not allowed fuel coupons and had to store the vehicle away in the garage until the war was over. There were very few of those in Fradley at that time. The Bell Bridge garage, which was owned by Mr. Alf Shearer, supplied petrol and carried out repairs to the few motor vehicles in the village.

The first bus to Lichfield each morning did not arrive at the end of Fradley Lane on Rykneld Street until 10.45am, so most people owned bicycles, which were used daily by those who travelled out of the village to work.

My mother and father had decided to move and live in Fradley in 1936, to reduce the time my dad spent on a bike riding to and from work. My sister, Joyce and myself were born in Springhill Cottages, near to The Boat Inn at Muckley Corner, on the Lichfield to Walsall road. At that time, Dad was travelling twelve miles each way to and from John Bannister's yard, a building contractor in Alrewas. He had worked in Fradley, helping to build four houses for Mrs. Annie Booth, one of which he managed to rent from her, which we came to live in when I was two years old and my sister Joyce, still a baby.

We were fortunate that the house, built in 1934, had electricity and mains water laid on. It was very modern, compared to most of the other houses in the village. Being semi-detached, my mother was able to give a knock on the party wall to let our neighbour, Mrs. Harcombe, know that she had some news to tell her and they would then meet up at the rear fence. The fences were quite low, however, so I was able to jump over to play with another friend of mine, Terry, who lived in the next pair of houses.

Most of the other houses in the village were lit with oil lamps and had outdoor lavatories without flushing or drainage systems. They were either earth closets or had a bucket below a wooden seat which required emptying weekly.

A hole was dug in the garden and the contents of the bucket tipped into it, before being covered with soil. I occasionally helped my pal Gel carry out the chore at his house, after his dad had left to join the Army. It was a very smelly operation and I was thankful that I did not have the job to do at home after my own dad had also been called up into the Army.

During the summer holidays, I occasionally stayed at the house of my aunt and uncle, who lived at Shire Oak, near Walsall Wood. My uncle drove a lorry to deliver bricks to building sites. Sometimes he let me go with him, if he was not starting too early in the day. It gave me the opportunity of seeing parts of the Midlands which I would not otherwise have seen. The alternative was to be ordered about by my older cousin, Muriel. She was not used to boys' games.

We usually played schools, Muriel being the teacher of course and me being the unruly pupil who had to stand most of the time in the corner, with my hands above my head. As we got older, we became good friends and in fact, she took me to see the sea for the first time, at the age of eleven, by way of a coach trip to Rhyl.

During a night air raid, my uncle called us up to go into the air raid shelter, which was built into a bank of earth in the front garden and was used by neighbours as well as family. I was not used to getting dressed during raids, as at home I had only to get out of bed and go under the staircase. Somehow that night, I managed to put my trousers on back to front, which was most uncomfortable when I sat down in the shelter and most embarrassing when the other people found out.

My dad's mother and father lived in a small cottage at the bottom of Shire Oaks hill. My dad used to take me occasionally on Sunday a afternoon, by bus, to see them. Sometimes Grandad could be seen staggering down the hill from the pub, having had a couple of pints too much for his own good. I often covered over my eyes, thinking that he was going to fall under a passing vehicle. He always managed to negotiate the way home and would get very excited when he saw us.

Grandma would always have a roaring fire, even in the summer. She made a lot of fuss when we arrived, scurrying around, continually making cups of tea.

Grandad was proud to take us the full length of his vegetable garden, explaining which were early potatoes and how big the onions and carrots were. He also kept a dozen or so rabbits in pens within the pigsty and an old tin with a few pennies stuck in a hole in the wall. He only had one tooth in his mouth and although he may not have been able to chew properly, he could certainly drink.

Fig 8: German Luftwaffe Aerial Photograph of Fradley Airfield taken on 4 October 1940. Key: 1) Hangars 2) Runways 3) Air Raid Shelters 4) Barracks. The photograph, which appeared in the Lichfield Mercury, was loaned to the paper by Mr. Geoffrey Powell. It originally belonged to Mr. Bertram Barlow, Lichfield undertaker, who obtained it from a German airman.

Although the German bomber pilots would have liked to drop a few bombs on the airfield at Fradley, they did not manage to do so. In fact the nearest bomb landed in the middle of a field, on the opposite side of the road to Bagnall Farm. It rattled a few windows in the village, but no one was hurt. Far more British bombs exploded on the airfield. It was fortunate that although the German Luftwaffe had aerial photographs of Fradley, taken during daylight, their bombers were unable to find it during their night time raids.

During the raids on Birmingham and Coventry, from my bedroom window, I could see a red glow in the night sky, a reflection from the fires below.

I was excited at the thought of a pilot coming to live with us, but alas, when our lodger arrived, I was disappointed to find that he was just an aircraft fitter.

I was keen to find out from him what sort of aeroplanes would be coming to Fradley. He just grinned and told me to mind my own business. My dad explained that perhaps the man thought that I was doing a bit of spying for the Germans. At the time I felt quite upset that I should be considered a likely traitor. I think now that Dad and this new lodger were having a little joke between themselves at my expense.

It was not long, however, before I was able to see for myself the type of aircraft arriving at Fradley. There seemed to be a continuous flow once the tarmac runways had been laid.

The noise of engines from overhead aircraft even drowned the sound of the school band.

The end of the main runway on the airfield was only a couple of hundred metres from the school and almost in line with the playground, so aircraft taking off or landing were so low that the pilot could be easily seen.

During the early days some of the planes were yellow in colour and were obviously for use in training air crew, but within a few weeks, a variety of different planes, both fighters and bombers, painted black on the lower parts and camouflaged with dark green and brown paint on the top of the fuselage and wings. Most of them had red, white and blue circles on the sides of the fuselage, denoting that they were British and letters and numbers, showing which squadron they belonged to.

My friend John, who lived at the shop and was a few years older than me, managed to get an aircraft recognition book, so we were soon able to distinguish a Wellington bomber from a Hurricane fighter and by recording their registration numbers, we were able to determine how many times each aircraft took off and landed at the airfield each day. Most flights did not did not last very long, so each pilot quickly got used to the same scene each time around. Eventually they started to return our hand-waving from the playground.

It was soon learned that Fradley was to be a training and

Fig 9: Returning Wellington bomber crew; photo courtesy of Mr Geoffrey Powell and the Lichfield Mercury.

maintenance unit, to start with anyway, which seemed quite logical as we were so far away from the south coast, where any attack was likely to be.

Unfortunately, there were numerous accidents involving aircraft taking off or landing.

At that time, at least one aircraft a week crashed at Fradley, most of them being Wellington bombers. Some aircrew had a shock, after engine failure on taking off, that the plane would belly land into the canal at the end of the runway.

Although it was intended mainly to train aircrew and service aircraft, when raids over Germany required greater numbers, Wellington bombers from Fradley joined the main group, notably on what was known as the "thousand bomber raids" on the German towns of Hamburg and Cologne.

The news of a 'prang' (the RAF wartime word for a crash), quickly spread around my friends and providing it happened outside the perimeter of the aerodrome and it wasn't being guarded, we were soon all over it, picking up souvenirs.

Fig. 10: Graves of aircrew buried in Fradley churchyard

Fig. 11: Wellington bomber

There was always a danger that we would pick up live ammunition, of course, so I was constantly being warned by my mother not to go near to the damaged aircraft.

Sometimes the impact of a crash would cause the plane to catch fire and if live ammunition was being carried, the heat would set off a series of bangs, when bullets and cannon shells would fly anywhere. As the fuel tanks exploded, a large cloud of black smoke would rise above the burning aircraft.

One day, my friend Ned Smith and myself were in the farmyard at Bycars Farm having a break from potato picking and enjoying our sandwiches, when we heard the spluttering sound of a plane with engine trouble. We ran to a spot where we could see the aircraft, only to realise that it was very low and nowhere near the flight path to make a landing on the runway. One wing was cut off after hitting the top of a poplar tree in front of the Bull's Head public house and fell into the main road. The aeroplane, a Manchester bomber, crashed into a nearby field, narrowly missing a row of houses on the road junction with Fradley Lane. As Ned lived in the end one, his immediate reaction was concern for the safety of his mother. As we ran across the field to get a better view, we could see that the plane had already burst into flames and that ammunition had started to explode. Fortunately, it missed the houses by about a hundred metres, leaving a sheet of outer canvas on the roof of Ned's house. None of the crew were able to escape before the fuel tanks exploded, sending a big plume of black smoke across the main road. Most of the crashes resulted in loss of life owing to the difficulty of access in and out of the bombers.

A considerable number of those killed were members of the Royal Australian Air Force, some of them being buried in Fradley churchyard. A funeral service was held in the church, when sometimes as many as four or five coffins would be carried in, each draped with the flag of their own country. I would be asked to go from school into the church to pump air into the organ in order that the organist could play music for the congregation to sing hymns, not that there was a great number of people attending. There were usually six bearers to each coffin, half a dozen airmen, armed with rifles, forming a guard of honour, two or three officers and the RAF padre. Some of the villagers would attend, to pay their respects, if the news of a military funeral was made known in advance.

After the service, the coffins were carried shoulder-high to the grave, where the men in the guard of honour would fire three times over the grave, with blank ammunition of course.

If the padre was seen in the village, it usually meant that bad news was about to be given to someone about a death on the airfield. I watched him go to our next door neighbours' house to inform a lady who was staying there, that her husband had been killed earlier that day.

A rear gunner of a Wellington bomber, who had lodged with us, was killed shortly after being posted to another airfield.

Chapter 3

THE QUIET little village of Fradley, which had previously been a mostly farming community where the fastest vehicle had been a horse and trap, was lost for ever.

By late 1940 there was constant aircraft noise, both day and night. Fradley was now definitely at war!

I remember my childhood as a very exciting time, with the growth of the airfield seeming to dominate my life. However, I still found time to do all the other things that young boys were expected to do, like fishing for tiddlers and sticklebacks in the streams or canal, playing games in the fields and around the farmyards, or doing a bit of scrumping in someone's orchard. The sense that I most remember is that of almost constant hunger. So a couple of apples usually satisfied the pang for a short time. Quite regularly, I was caught red-handed, usually because I would attempt to get an extra apple or pear after the warning call had been sounded by one of my pals. It would result in a telling-off by the owner and a clout from my mother when she found out.

I even got into trouble for stealing cow manure. It was springtime and my father had started to dig the garden and plant seed potatoes. I was always keen to help, but often got in the way, so to transfer my interest elsewhere, he suggested that I took my little wheelbarrow into the road, to collect any manure dropped by the horses and cows which had been driven along earlier in the day. There was usually enough to fill my wheelbarrow, but on this day someone else had already collected it for their own garden. Not to be outdone, I knew where there was plenty of fresh cow muck. In Watson's field, of course, where the cows spent most of their day. I had almost filled my wheelbarrow, when Mr. Norman Watson spotted me. He asked me what I thought I was doing.

"Collecting some muck for my dad's garden," I proudly told him.

Quite calmly, he explained that the manure was in his field and therefore belonged to him. He said that I could take home the contents of my wheelbarrow and told me to tell my dad that he would deliver a cartload for him later that day. We had a super crop of potatoes later in the year.

Air raid shelters were constructed for use in the event of a bombing raid by German aircraft. Most families dug a hole in the garden, deep enough to stand in, with a roof built to withstand anything falling, usually of heavy timbers covered with soil and turfed over.

We were allocated what was known as a Morrison shelter, which was to be erected within the house and resembled a table (see illustration). It consisted of a heavy steel sheet supported on thick angle iron legs, with smaller angle trimmers bolted to the legs to prevent it from falling over. A sheet of steel mesh was laid across the trimmers to form a bed. When a mattress was laid on top of the mesh, there was just enough room to crawl in, below the steel top.

The idea was to dispense with the wooden table which was normally being used to eat our meals upon, however Dad estimated that the wooden floor in the house was not strong enough to carry the weight of the shelter together with the weight of the family, so it was never erected and

Fig 12: Illustration from the booklet 'How to put up your Morrison Shelter', issued by the Ministry of Home Security in 1941.

leaned, within the garage, against the wall for the duration of the war. Eventually, years after, the steel sheet was used on the bottom of the local coal lorry, where I believe a hole had started to form.

During the nightly air raids, we resorted to the alcove below the stairs, where there was a permanently made-up bed on the floor. My mother never did fancy putting her tablecloth on top of an iron table.

A brick air raid shelter was built in the school playground, backing on to the church railings. It had a reinforced concrete roof, a wooden slatted door at each end, benches running down the length of each side and a small end compartment housing a toilet, consisting of a board with a hole in it, over a bucket.

Air raid practice was carried out each week. Before the shelter was completed we had to get under our desks when teacher blew her whistle and shouted "AIR RAID". After completion of the shelter, we walked quickly outside, sat in the shelter and put on our gas masks for about ten minutes.

Some children hated these practices and complained that they could not breathe in their rubber respirator. I used to practise at home to see how long I could remain with it on my face.

Your own personal gas mask was kept in a small cardboard box and had to be carried everywhere you went. Within a few months of them being issued, an additional filter, coloured green had to be fitted. It was the responsibility of the ARP personnel to tape the filter on and check that the respirator was airtight.

Each one was tested by asking the owner to put on the mask and to breathe in whilst a piece of paper was placed under the filter. If the suction of the breath could support the paper, it was assumed that the gas mask fitted correctly.

Brown sticky tape was stuck across all the panes of glass in the windows of the school and most houses in a crossed pattern, looking very much like the union flag. The object was that if the glass was shattered by an explosion, it would be retained by the tape and would not fall within the room.

Fortunately there was never an air raid over Fradley during school hours. It was always night time when the enemy bombers came over. The air raid warning signal would sound, usually just after dark and often before we had finished our evening meal. I would put as much on my plate as I could and take it with me below the staircase -- not even a German bomber would stop me from eating.

It was quite surprising how we got used to the interruptions. We quickly began to recognise the difference in sound of a German aircraft overhead and one of our own, sometimes before the wail of the siren started. It was always reassuring to hear the continuous tone of the "all clear" signal.

In the early stages of the war, before joining the Army, my father was a member of the local ARP (Air Raid Precautionary Force). It was part of his responsibility to walk around the village after nightfall to ensure that each house had blackout blinds properly fixed, in order to prevent any light being seen by enemy aircraft above.

The wardens met each night at a small brick hut in Church Lane, at the junction of Fradley Lane. The hut was equipped with a bed, stretchers to carry anyone who might be wounded, stirrup pumps for pumping water in case of fire and a number of first aid kits.

The hut was also used by the ladies of the village who met up weekly to distribute wool for knitting jumpers, socks and gloves for members of the forces. I was often ordered by my mother to stand with my arms stretched out in front of me, onto which she would hang a skein of wool, whilst she wound it into balls. I learned to knit at school, so once I had proved myself, Mum allowed me to knit a scarf with navy blue wool, which I understood would be sent to a sailor. The ladies would put a note in with the woollens, wishing the person the best of luck and hoping that the item of clothing would help to keep them warm during the winter.

Occasionally on Sundays, the wardens, together with the local branch of the Home Guard, practised the procedure for action to be taken in the event of a serious bombing raid taking place. The Home Guard would stand in the ditches around the village with rifles at the ready to ward off any attack. I think it was thought that there might be a parachute drop by the enemy in an attempt to capture the aerodrome.

Some civilians were asked to fake an injury, to give the first aid people practice and small fires were started on steel sheets to allow the wardens to train in the use of their stirrup pumps. There was a stirrup pump and galvanised bucket left permanently in our garage. It came in very handy to water the garden during dry weather.

The government motto of "Dig for Victory", was taken literally in our village.

Every family planted as many vegetables as possible. Even areas which had been flower borders before the war started, were now being converted into vegetable plots. Although I was still young, I learned from my father how to sow seeds and plant potatoes, which was most useful to me after Dad been called up into the Army. With my mother's help, I managed to dig and plant most of the vegetable garden for four years, getting more proficient each year as I got older and gained more strength.

In fact, when my father returned home, I was resentful when he again took over control of the garden and made decisions about the layout.

He also reclaimed his bicycle and even his best pair of shoes, which I had often worn whilst he was away.

Collections of waste paper and scrap metal, known at the time as the "War Effort", were made around the village by a few of us boys. I had a small wooden wheelbarrow which my father had arranged to be made for me in the joiners' shop at Bannisters, where he worked, before the war started.

Any iron railings or fencing around houses were taken down and sent away with all other scrap metal, such as tins, old saucepans and steel tools which were no longer used.

The railings and gates around the church were about the only ones to remain.

There was a building at The Poplars Farm where all the paper and metal was deposited for collection each month.

One Saturday afternoon during the winter of 1940, I had been around The Moor, when I saw some of the older boys playing on the ice covering a pond. I talked them into letting me get on to the ice with them. They broke the ice all around the edge so that the centre became a floating ice raft. One of the boys pushed against the bank with a long stick, making the raft spin around in the middle of the pond. It was great fun until my dad suddenly appeared, riding his bike down the road towards us. I knew that I would be in trouble if he spotted me on the ice, so I decided to jump off onto the bank. Unfortunately, it was farther away than I thought. I fell well short and landed in the cold, dirty water.

One of the lads hauled me on to dry land just in time for me to waddle into the roadway in front of my dad, my short trousers sticking to my legs and my wellies full of water.

Dad didn't speak, he just pointed towards home. I have often thought since that he probably had difficulty in not laughing.

A WARTIME SCHOOLBOY: MEMORIES OF FRADLEY

I squelched my way along the roadway, pushing my little wheelbarrow, knowing that Dad was riding his bike slowly, a few yards behind, wondering what reaction I would get from him once we were within our own garden.

When passing the Barnes house, Mrs. Barnes, who was working in the garden, raised her head, acknowledged my father and commented that she was pleased to see young boys like me out collecting scrap paper for the war effort. Dad, of course smiled at her, made a polite remark but didn't, as I thought he might, suggest to her that she should have seen me a few minutes earlier up to my waist in pond water.

My mother was far from pleased when she saw me, standing shivering on the doorstep, my lower half covered with dark mud.

Chapter 4

EACH WINTER we had prolonged hard frosts and snow falls which often cut off the village. As children we had great fun, but the farmers found it difficult to manage dairy herds when the grass in the fields was covered with a blanket of twelve inches (30cm.) of snow.

Getting the milk to the milk factory in Kings Bromley was a nightmare. In normal weather a wagon from the dairy travelled around the farms delivering empty churns and collecting the full churns of milk, which were normally left outside the farm gate, often on a raised platform for ease of loading by the driver, who was usually alone.

During the winter of 1939-40, however, the snow was too deep for the wagon to travel along the lanes so the number of churns of milk had started to build up on all of the farms and most farmers had run out of empties. So it was decided to take the milk on four-wheeled drays, pulled by two horses harnessed to each. The men attending them all carried shovels to dig the snow from under the wheels, each time that they were bogged down. My father, who could not do his normal job of work, laying bricks, owing to the low temperatures, went along with them, to give a helping hand.

The convoy started from the village in the early morning, proceeded around the various farms collecting the

Fig 13: Mum, Dad, sister Joyce and myself at 'The Mount'

milk and then set off towards Kings Bromley via Hay End Lane, Fradley Junction and Orgreave. It was nightfall when they returned home.

During very cold weather, my parents found it necessary to place oil stoves around the house wherever water pipes were likely to freeze. Most winters, however, a pipe burst somewhere and flooded part of the house.

I did not have a birthday celebration as a child; my birthday being in January meant that a plumber would be either thawing pipes so that we could have water or repairing one after the thaw had revealed a burst.

There was usually a roaring fire in the living room, which had an oven alongside and a trivet, on which a kettle would stand, constantly boiling.

The other rooms in the house were quite cold during wintertime. To warm my bed, my mother would wrap a house brick, which had been warmed in the oven, in a small piece of old sheet or blanket. It helped to warm my feet, but made them quite sore if I happened to kick it during the night, especially when I was suffering with chilblains.

At Christmas, my mother used to hang up a holly branch from the ceiling so that together with my sister, I would put onto it small pieces of cotton wool, resembling snow. We cut newspaper into strips, painted it in contrasting colours and made paper chains to hang across the living room. Our presents amounted to no more than a penny and some fruit, either an orange or a banana, whichever was available. As we didn't see fruit from overseas very often, it was our luxury at Christmas.

Letters were delivered by a postman in a van from Lichfield, who also collected the outgoing mail from the post office. During the worst winters, it was arranged that someone met the postman at the junction of the main road (A38) and Fradley Lane each morning to collect the post and hand over the outgoing mail. A similar arrangement was made to collect the daily newspapers.

Hardy's shop and post office proved to be the centre where most things were organised in the village. The only public telephone was situated in a kiosk in front of the shop and as most people in the village didn't have their own phone, it was well used. The shop supplied most things, so the villagers generally met up there or picked up any messages being passed around. Newspapers were delivered from there by village boys.

I started my first newspaper round when I was about eight years old. The inner village round involved only about a dozen houses nearest to the shop, was usually carried out by the youngest boy and could be delivered each day before going to school. Every rear door to the houses remained unlocked, so I would call out "Paper!", as I opened the door and usually left it on the kitchen table.

A WARTIME SCHOOLBOY: MEMORIES OF FRADLEY

The villagers trusted each other, in fact friends who visited our house usually just knocked the door and walked in, without needing to be invited.

Wartime conditions encouraged people to cooperate with each other. A number of women were left with young children when their husbands were called into the forces. Some grouped together in the evenings when enemy air raids were taking place, often in shelters. There were no public air raid shelters in the village, as the small population was so widespread, so most houses had built their own facility.

I remember well the day that my father left home to join the Army. He had arranged to meet another man, Mr. Leedham, who lived in Alrewas and was going to the same training barracks. They travelled by train from Alrewas railway station to Shrewsbury, where they were to join the Shropshire Light Infantry. Dad gave me a lift on the crossbar of his bicycle to Alrewas and I rode his bike back home, after saying goodbye to him.

At that time I was very excited to be allowed to ride his bike, having little thought for the fact that he would be away from home for the next four years.

Although our country was now well involved in World War II, each November 11th at 11am., two minutes' silence was observed during school lessons, in memory of those who lost their lives during the First World War.

Members of the British Legion, who were either too old or unfit to serve in the current war, held a remembrance service in the church on the nearest Sunday. The RAF were always represented by about a dozen airmen and an officer, who marched from the airfield.

It was a welcome relief for me, having a change to the normal boring service, which I had to attend to pump air into the organ. A wreath of red poppies was placed on the small memorial stone on the wall near to where I sat at the end of the organ, by a member of the British Legion.

Fradley School was used, after school hours, for other activities organised by the villagers. On Friday evenings there would sometimes be a whist drive and occasionally, a dance was held afterwards. The RAF would send two or three men with musical instruments, to form a band and any others who were not on duty, together with members of the WAAFS, who were now also based at Fradley and billeted at Streethay, would come to dance and enjoy an evening in the village. The rough boarded floor was not the ideal surface to dance upon, so someone would scatter soap flakes on it to reduce the friction. However, when we children returned to school on Monday morning, it was so slippery that we could use it to slide upon, often on our bottoms. It would remain polished until the cleaning lady gave it its weekly scrub.

After a couple of years being taught by Miss Dobson, she retired and was replaced by Mrs. McKnight, who was the wife of the headmaster at Alrewas School. She walked each morning from Alrewas to Fradley and back again after school had closed in the afternoon, summer and winter whatever the weather. I found her to be quite different to Miss Dobson, and although strict, very kind. As she had children of her own, I think she understood young kids very well and got the best out of us.

Shortly after reaching eight years old, in 1942, I was told that I was now old enough to go to Alrewas School. I was no longer an infant.

Alrewas C of E School
1942 - 1945

Chapter 5

MY FRIENDS, all being older than me, had been at Alrewas School for up to a couple of years before I started. I was no longer to be called by my first name of 'Colin'. For the rest of my school life I was known by my nickname of 'Rusty'. Even my mother called me by my nickname most of the time.

Although I was tall for my age, I was very inexperienced at fighting to protect myself. I quickly found that most boys who I had never met before were friendly, but a few were always prepared to challenge me to a fight. Fortunately, my pal Gel was usually nearby and didn't hesitate to threaten any aggressor who appeared to be squaring up to me.

We walked each day to Alrewas School, often meeting Mrs. McKnight walking the other way towards Fradley School. We always wished her "Good morning" and touched our caps. Most of us boys wore caps in those days and often one of them would be snatched by an older boy and thrown over the hedge.

There was always an initiation ceremony of some sort for new pupils. In my case it happened on the way home from school on the first afternoon. In the middle of a field, I was held down whilst hawthorn berries were pushed into my ears.

Fig 14: Alrewas C of E School

It was nothing serious but nevertheless was a bit frightening for an eight-year-old, not knowing what was likely to happen next.

On the way home from school we played a variety of games. One of my favourites was to imagine that we were in either the Army or the Air Force. My friend Gel, being older than me, usually played the part of a high-ranking officer, who marched us younger ones up and down the roadway. We had our rank, in the form of stripes, pips or rings, marked on our clothes with chalk.

After being 'promoted' numerous times, the sleeves of my jacket or pullover would be covered with chalk, much to the annoyance of my mother when I arrived home, especially if I was later than usual, when she was expecting me to come home promptly to run some errands for her.

Occasionally we were sent back to Alrewas, to take shoes or boots to the cobblers to be repaired. In addition to the leather sole, I had metal studs put onto mine in order that they would not wear out so quickly. After dark they made lovely sparks when scraped along the pebbled roadway.

Gel's mum sometimes sent him to Hart's garage in Main Street Alrewas, to take the accumulator battery to be re-charged. As they hadn't got electricity in their house, it was the only way to power the wireless. The lighting was in the form of oil lamps, which gave out a very good light. I was fascinated to see Gel's dad light his cigarette by putting the end of it in the heat of the flame over the top of the glass globe.

I spent quite a lot of time at my friend Gel's house. We built a den in a clump of lilac trees at the end of his garden and used it as a hideout for all sorts of games from cow-boys and Indians to war games. Sometimes when I timed it well, I could have a meal at home and then run over to Gel's house in time for his mum to call him in for his din-ner. She always invited me to have some, which of course I never refused.

When she was baking, she would call to us and offer a couple of jam tarts. They tasted wonderful when still warm. She made her own jam from the apple and plum trees in their garden. His mum threatened not to give us any more jam tarts one day, after we had broken down one of the plum trees by swinging on the clothes line which was fastened to the tree. There was an almighty cracking sound as it fell on top of us, giving us no chance of escap-ing before Gel's mum saw us.

During the summer months we usually walked across the fields to school, passing the cottages at Cowhill, over the stile adjacent to the conker tree, across Daisy Lane and over Walkfield, around the cricket pitch to Kent's Bridge. It was often too wet during the winter months to risk walking across the fields. Except for Walkfield, which cut off half a mile or so, we would stay on the roadway around Bagnall corner.

Mr. J. R. McKnight, the headmaster, would often be in

the playground, smoking his pipe, when we arrived. He would inspect our boots for cleanliness and having walked across a field was no excuse for them being dirty.

I regularly wiped the mud from my boots with my handkerchief or rubbed them up the back of my stockings, if I could see "The Gaffer" in the distance.

When there had been a hard frost for a week or two and the canal was well frozen, which happened often in the winters of the 1940s, we would complete our journey from Walkfield on the ice, under Kent's Bridge rather than over it. We were not allowed on to the canal until the ice had been tested by Mr. McKnight, who enjoyed having a slide on it as much as the children.

One morning, however, the temperature had risen overnight and the ice had started to thaw. Two of my friends, Pont and Frank, were brave enough to walk on to the ice to test it. Unfortunately it cracked when they were too far away from the bank to scramble back and both of them fell through it into the cold water. They managed to get out and scrambled up the bank, dripping wet and freezing with cold.

Pont decided not face the wrath of the headmaster and ran home to Fradley. Frank opted to face his punishment and was sent to the headmaster's house to take off his clothes to dry them in front of an open fire.

The headmaster was keen to see us enjoy outdoor activities. The older boys spent one afternoon each week in the garden, digging and planting vegetables, whilst the older girls were taught cookery.

One afternoon each week was spent playing games, in my case football during the winter months and cricket in the summer. We played in the playing field alongside the canal at the rear of the vicarage garden. There was no grass at all in the centre of the field, owing to constant wear by numerous boots, daily scuffing up the turf.

A WARTIME SCHOOLBOY: MEMORIES OF FRADLEY

Mr. McKnight often joined in the cricket matches with the boys and gave advice on how to hold the bat correctly or how to bowl a "googly". He also made the umpiring decisions if there was any argument as to whether the batsman was out. One lovely warm day, when he was more interested in lighting his pipe than watching the cricket, a lad fielding on the boundary misjudged his throw and knocked the pipe out of the boss's mouth with the cricket ball. Both teams remained unusually silent, waiting for the repercussion – which didn't come.

"Carry on boys, it was an accident," he called.

I think he realised how fortunate he was that his spectacles weren't broken and pushed into his eyes. The boy breathed a sigh of relief that the headmaster had been so sporting about it.

I was ten years old when the invasion of Europe started. My mother was very concerned about whether or not my father was involved on 6th June 1944, when the news broke of the first landings by allied troops in Normandy.

He had come home without warning for a few days' leave, just a few weeks before and didn't seem to know much about where he was going to be posted when he returned to his regiment.

Unfortunately, I didn't see very much of him on that occasion, as I was confined to bed with pneumonia. Dr. Russian always seemed to order me to bed for about a couple of weeks, what ever the illness. I had every complaint during my childhood: mumps, measles, chicken pox and even a complaint called nettle rash, which wasn't caused by falling into a bed of nettles but felt very much like it.

Childhood illnesses were passed from one friend to another around the village. The doctor used to say to my mother, "How many more of his friends have I to call on today? If he has caught it, I expect two or three others have it as well!"

The medicine he made up for us had to be collected from the surgery at Alrewas and always tasted like paraffin.

Mum used to lay the newspaper out on the table each morning and explain to me with the aid of the numerous maps published, where the allied armies had advanced to. It seemed an age to me before they advanced far into France.

My mother was not a person who got over-excited at all, but on the morning that the postman opened the door and shouted that he had got a letter from Dad, even she couldn't open it quick enough. It had been written two weeks previously from the Isle of Wight, before he had boarded a troop ship to follow the early invasion forces.

Mother was relieved to hear from him and the letters came regularly, about one each week, after that. We didn't see him again until the war was well over and he returned in 1946 to be demobbed.

Chapter 6

AS I GOT older, I was allowed to deliver both newspapers and groceries to the outlying areas of the village, Fradley Junction and even on to the aerodrome. The longer rounds could only be covered by schoolboys at weekends, however. During weekdays, these rounds were carried out by a man with a van from the shop, or in later years by my friend Gel, when he worked full-time at the shop.

There were few cars in the village. Some of the farmers owned them, but they were restricted during the war to use them only for essential journeys. Petrol was rationed, the allowance being small and only made to those people who could prove it was essential to use a vehicle, so most families had their groceries delivered from the shop by the delivery boy on a bike.

I often did the deliveries after school and on Saturdays, particularly to the outlying areas. Most housewives had an order book, in which they wrote a list of the items of grocery required, which they left at the shop a couple of days before they wanted them delivered.

The goods would be put into a cardboard box and loaded into the basket over the small front wheel of the bike. All goods were rationed, so none of the boxes were very heavy.

The main problem for any delivery boy was being chased by dogs. Most houses and all farms had dogs, usually free to roam around. I tried to get onto a friendly basis with them, but there was always one who would fancy a nip at my ankles. I even put sheets of cardboard into my socks to prevent them drawing blood.

If any of Mr. Hardy's customers ordered oatmeal to feed fowl, I was allowed to weigh it into large paper bags in the wooden store shed at the rear of the shop. I liked the different smells in the shed, ground oats, oatmeal and paraffin.

The classes at Alrewas School were known as 'standards'. There was an infants' class, but of course children being transferred from Fradley were already eight years old, so we started our education there in Standard Two.

There were five classrooms in addition to the infants' room, although the seniors, who left the school when they reached fourteen years old, were taught at the end of one of the rooms, by the headmaster.

There were cloak rooms for both girls and boys, with a range of hat and coat hooks and a few wash hand basins. The toilets were again away from the main school building, in order that the smell from them didn't filter into the teaching areas. At least the W.C.s were connected to a drain and had water flushing systems.

The rooms were heated by a central heating system run from a boiler in an outbuilding, with water passing through large pipes around the rooms into cast-iron radiators. They were big enough to sit upon and were very welcome when the weather was cold. The headmaster ensured that the boiler was stoked well with coke before school started each morning. Always the recognisable smell of Mr. McKight's pipe floated around the classrooms first thing each morning. I always thought that it was quite a pleasant smell, though also a warning to beware that "The Gaffer" was not far away.

Miss Mary Ward was my teacher for the first year. In

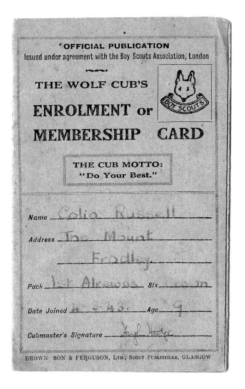

Fig 15: Enrolment Card for the Cubs

addition to teaching, Miss Ward was also Bagheera in the Alrewas Wolf Cub Pack (now called Cub Scouts). The vicar, the Rev. Hugh Hodge, was the scout master and also Akela in the Cub pack.

There were few men left in the villages to run organisations like the Scouts and youth clubs, so the vicar doubled up on a few jobs.

I joined the Cubs shortly after starting Alrewas school. Weekly meetings were held at the vicarage, where various activities were arranged to encourage team play and friendship. During the summer months we spent a lot of time in the fields alongside the River Trent and during the winter months, games were played in one of the rooms in the vicarage which was reserved for the Scouts and Cubs.

The girls also had a room for Guide and Brownie meetings.

During Cub meetings I learned to clean shoes properly, to administer some basic first aid and to carry out a bit of simple cooking. With food being rationed, however, we were not allowed to cook more than vegetables, which could be begged from local farmers. Roast potatoes were on the menu more often than anything else.

Although I walked to school, my mother allowed me to use my dad's bike to return to Alrewas for any after-school activity.

During school holidays and on Saturdays in September most boys went into the fields to assist the farmers to pick potatoes. I earned a few shillings in that way to help my mother to feed me. We took sandwiches and a bottle of

Fig 16: Alrewas Wolf Cub Pack with Miss Mary Ward

cold tea to kill the thought of hunger until we returned home in the evening. The farmer usually allowed us to take a couple of potatoes home each evening. It was only natural for us to select the largest that we could find.

It was our normal practice for me to put my spud into the hot coals of the fire and bake it until the skin was black, cut it through the middle and hope that Mum would allow me to have a little bit of butter to melt on top.

If we were working in the fields owned by the Watson family, Mrs. Watson often invited us into the farmhouse to have something to eat. We would sit in front of a roaring hot fire in the range. The coal would be glowing red when we would be invited to put in our potatoes to bake them. Each person knew their own spud and kept a close eye on it in the glowing embers.

On one memorable occasion, John, the eldest there, decided that his potato was cooked and duly took it out with the fire tongs, put it on to a plate, cut it and put on a knob of butter. At this point my young sister, Joyce, argued with John that it was her potato that he was going to eat. When she realised that he was not going agree, she spat right into the middle of it, exclaiming, "It's mine now!" I think John was too flabbergasted to do anything about it.

I spent a great deal of my time on farms during my childhood. There were at least eight farms in Fradley at that time. I was attracted to Marsh Farm more than any other, mainly because my mum and dad were friendly with Mr. and Mrs. Watson and I liked being around the farm and in the fields with their sons, John and Frank, who were both older than me.

I learned to do other jobs in addition to picking potatoes. Cutting kale, often a daily job done during the winter, I always considered to be the worst. The kale was at least waist high, wet or frozen. It had to be chopped through near to the ground and thrown on to the cart, later to be distributed to the cows in the field. The centre pith of the kale stalk was quite nice to eat, although devouring too much ensured that you went to the loo more often the following day.

I also learned how to put a milking machine on to a cow, although when asked to do it, I always chose a quiet one who was less likely to kick. The friendly ones were well known to me. Each cow had a name, which was remembered like that of a friend. A bowl of cow cake granules was tipped into the manger in front of each cow at milking time. It was their reward for giving up their milk to the machine. I often ate a few lumps myself to help stem the pangs of hunger. It tasted like dry grass.

Blocks of salt were placed in the fields or fixed to the cowshed wall for the cows to lick. I occasionally took a lick myself, but instead of curing hunger it gave me a thirst, so to satisfy that problem I would have a drink out of the animals' trough. The most satisfying drink of water on a hot day, was a gulp of the lovely cold water that came through the brass tap in the outhouse at The Poplars Farm. Many times, I drank so much of it that my stomach ached.

I loved to be around the horses. Before tractors were brought on to the farms, horses were used to pull the carts, plough the fields and pull the binders cutting the corn at harvest time.

At Marsh Farm, the Watson family had some lovely horses. Dinky was a small friendly mare, who was used for any duty, from trotting along pulling the two-wheeled trap, to heavy work in the fields. Ted, I remember as being more temperamental and the one that I was most afraid of. Gordon, a large heavy stallion, could do any job that he was asked to do but was also a most gentle and friendly horse. All of them could be ridden when the opportunity arose, usually to and from the fields.

I often went with Frank to take a horse to be shod. The

blacksmith's forge in Main Street at Alrewas was always very warm, the ideal place to be in winter. The smith worked to a rhythm, his hammer bouncing on the anvil constantly, with an occasional diversion to hit the shoe – which had already been brought up to a very high temperature in the coke furnace – moulding it to the shape of the horse's hoof.

When he was satisfied that the shoe was about the correct shape, he would place it onto the horse's hoof, held between his own knees. The red-hot shoe would burn into the hoof creating a cloud of pungent smoke. When the blacksmith was happy that it fitted correctly, he would dip the shoe into a bath of water to cool it and then fix it to the hoof with about half a dozen nails which pierced the hoof, each one being twisted to break it off on the top surface of the hoof. Amazingly the horse didn't seem to feel any pain at all.

We walked miles with either horses or cows. During summer months heifers were moved from Fradley to a field at Croxall, a walk of about two miles. When we crossed the level crossing at The Roddidge, one of us boys would place a halfpenny on the railway line and collect it on our return, by then flattened out to twice the size by a passing train. When the cattle were safely driven into the field, we would often strip down to our underpants and have a cool dip in the River Mease, before wending our way home.

Watching the corn being cut during the summer holidays was most enjoyable. As the binder gradually reduced the area left in the middle of the field, the rabbits would dash out and attempt to dodge the men with guns, who were hoping to shoot a couple for dinner.

After the corn had been carted into the farmyard and stacked in a rick, it was time for the thrashing machine to visit the farm. The thrashing drum was towed behind a steam engine, by Mr. Jack Jones, around the village, from one farm to another. The farmers often moved around also, helping each other to complete the harvest. I always found it exciting to follow the big machine trundling along, belching out steam.

The farmyard and fields were ideal places to play games. "Kick the can" was often played around the farm buildings. All the boys except for one hid in the buildings or behind the ricks, whilst the person who was chosen to be "on" had to find one of them, shout their name and kick the can before anyone else. Sometimes the can would get filled with water, unknown to the lad who was to kick it, causing added fun.

The game of "Fox and Hounds" was played over several fields. The players would decide who was going to be the fox and he would be allowed five minutes to escape and hide wherever he liked. The hounds would pursue him and attempt to catch him. Sometimes the game would last until after darkness had fallen with the fox not even being seen, let alone caught.

On the hot summer days, with my mate Gel, I used to go swimming in the canal. Well, he soon learned the art of swimming, but I could not keep afloat long enough to take more than one stroke.

Our mothers were not happy about us getting into the canal, so we had to smuggle the two bathing costumes from the outside wash house at Gel's, where they were normally kept, and return them afterwards without being seen. We didn't have a towel, so we dried ourselves by running around, before getting dressed.

Chapter 7

ONE LATE afternoon, when we, together with some of our other pals were in the canal, we spotted what looked like a strip of gold in the water. We had heard about gold being found in rivers in foreign countries, but didn't really expect there to be any in "the cut" at Fradley.

One lad shouted, "Gold! It's our lucky day!"

He thrust his arm deep into the water and lifted the bright nugget. "It's a bullet!" he declared.

It was – a 0.303-inch (7.7mm) live round... Grovelling in the mud for a few minutes proved that there were more than one. We unearthed several handfuls of the things. After a short council meeting, we decided to put as many rounds as we could into our pockets and take them into the village.

We found that when the pointed end of one of the bullets was pushed into a joint in a brick wall, the end could be broken off, exposing the inside. We stood a few on end along the top of a wall, lit the cordite which created a sparkling display, reminiscent of the fireworks which we had not seen since before the war started. The firework party ended abruptly when one of the rounds exploded and several mothers appeared on the scene.

PC 'Bobby' Baines was not too pleased, having to cycle from Alrewas to investigate where we had found the ammo and report it to the authorities on the airfield.

When tractors came into general use, I was big enough, if not old enough, to drive one. However, I pestered John Woolley, at Bycars farm, to let me have a go at steering the David Brown tractor. Reluctantly at first he allowed me to have a go in the field, and after a year or so of casual driving, I became quite good at it, so on some occasions it was easier to leave me on the tractor to move it on whilst one of the men loaded the hay or whatever was being carted behind.

One day, however, I misjudged turning and drove into the rick, breaking the cast iron grille in front of the radiator. I had an embarrassing few minutes explaining to Mr. Woolley how I had managed to do it.

During wartime, animals were killed on the farms to provide meat. It was not unusual for me to see cockerels have their necks broken, particularly at Christmas time. When I was old enough I learned to do it myself. I was never too keen at watching a pig killed. There was always a lot of blood and I was sometimes given the job at Bycars farm of standing near the gate, holding a yard broom and given instructions by the pig killer Mr. Albert Green, not to let any blood run off the yard. The pig was cut into sections, all of the hair scraped from it and hung from hooks on the kitchen ceiling.

One of my lasting memories of wartime was the fact that I always felt hungry. The moment I returned home from school, I would dive into the pantry to find something to eat. My mother had to hide food from my hungry eyes, otherwise the family rations would not last out the week. We had a bread bin which stood on the floor immediately inside the pantry door. I could usually bank on there being a crust of stale bread which to me tasted superb.

To give me a little variety, my mother would cut the crusts into various shapes, bake them very hard in the oven and give them to me when I complained of hunger. She called them "wartime biscuits" and because they had been baked so hard, they took longer than soft bread to eat.

During summer and autumn, I could usually find an attractive fruit tree. As we hadn't any trees in our garden it had to be that of someone else. I was often in trouble for being caught scrumping, usually from Watsons' orchard at the rear of The Poplars Farm.

On one occasion, I was on my way home from school with a group of friends, having walked across the fields from Alrewas, past the cottages on Cowhill into a field behind Marsh Farm. We knew that an apple tree in Daddy Barnes' garden overhung the hedge and that there were always windfall apples lying below.

On that particular afternoon we were surprised to find that there weren't any apples. Someone had beaten us to it and had already collected them. The looks of disappointment on some of our hungry faces prompted one enterprising member of our gang to suggest that we made a few more windfalls for ourselves. A stone was thrown which sailed up through the branches of the tree without even dislodging a single apple and crashed through the roof of a nearby greenhouse.

Instead of lying low behind the hedge, we panicked and made a run for it across the open field, leaving Daddy Barnes the opportunity of recognising the culprits. Within an hour, Mrs. Barnes was despatched by Daddy to inform the mothers of the vandals of their misdeed. I saw her talking to my mother at the gate and noticed Mother look round to see if I was within calling distance.

Although I was hiding in the shed, I knew that I was going to be in trouble when I had to return to the house.

"Perhaps best to face the music now," I thought and came out to meet an irate Mum who instructed me to go at six o'clock to see Daddy Barnes to apologise. My friends had all been given the same message, so we trooped down the road together, getting more afraid as we neared the Barnes household. As I was the youngest, I was told to go first to the door and knock. I didn't know which was worse, refusing to obey the older boys or face the wrath of Daddy Barnes as their leader.

My mind was made up for me when I was given a push from the back, the door opening at the same time.

"Come in!" he boomed, "Stand in a line!"

We stood stiffly in a single line in the hallway. I thought it best to keep my bottom pressed tightly against the wall. Less chance of me receiving an unexpected whack from his walking stick, which he always carried.

Daddy Barnes was a magistrate and used to dealing with delinquents. He strutted up and down the hallway in front of us, relating the damage in detail. Several sheets of glass had been broken in the roof of the greenhouse and a couple of bunches of prize grapes had been broken from the vine. "When the repairs have been completed, I shall send the bill to your parents for payment," he shouted.

"Now, get out! If you want any windfall apples in future come to the door and ask."

We couldn't get out quickly enough, almost knocking Daddy down in the process.

When we had reached the road, out of sight of the Barnes house window, one of my mates suggested that we should go back to the door, knock it and ask for some windfalls. There were no volunteers to do it, however.

It suddenly struck me at that time that I had now to explain to my mum that she was going to receive a bill for part of the cost of the damage. That was going to be very much more painful than the meeting with Mr. Barnes. I also realised that the few pennies which I was allowed to keep from my newspaper round would be sacrificed for months and months.

That bill for the damage was never sent to our mothers by

Daddy Barnes. He obviously realised that with most of the fathers being away from home in the forces, our mothers had barely enough money each week to feed us hungry kids.

However, the telling off was enough warning for us not to go near the apple trees in that garden again.

There were plenty of fruit trees elsewhere in the village which I still visited when hungry. With experience, I learned that I was less likely to be seen when I was alone or with only one friend rather than a group of us.

When the apple picking season was over, I usually resorted to digging up a few pig nuts to supplement my diet. The fields used for grazing the cows, some of which hadn't been ploughed for years, usually yielded an abundance of pig nuts a few inches below the turf, easily detected by the growth above the ground. I even attempted to eat horse chestnuts, but found them much too bitter. So I collected them to play conkers and baked a few in the oven, to harden them, hoping to win a few games.

If any pupil got into any sort of trouble outside of school hours, the headmaster, Mr. McKnight, would punish the culprits with a few strokes of the cane, so we had to be particularly careful.

My first taste of the cane came during a reading class, which Mr. McKnight was taking. He had noticed that I had been talking to the boy sitting next to me. The headmaster suddenly called out my name and told me to continue reading. I hadn't got a clue where he had left off but I didn't intend admitting it without having a guess. Hoping that I was going to be lucky, I started to read from the first line of the paragraph at the top of the right hand page. I had uttered only three or four words, when I sensed that there was some muffled sniggering coming from the remainder of the class. I was obviously reading from a page which had long been passed.

"Come out to the front of the class, Russell, and you

Venables."

As we both stumbled to the front, the headmaster picked up his cane from the teacher's desk.

"Hold out your hand," he said, as he pointed at me.

I wasn't sure whether it was better to go first or last but as Lou Venables didn't push forward to take first hit, knowing that he was more experienced at these things than I was, I guessed that I was going to regret having been first to arrive at the front of the class.

The following few seconds seemed an age to me. I had time to wonder what the experience would be like. Would it sting for long or would I be able to pass it off with a smile as I had seen older boys in the school do? Some of them, however, had the cane at least once a week and were proud to brag that they had more strokes of the "cosh" than anyone else. They also had advice on how to limit the pain by putting a strand of hair across the hand or lowering the hand as the cane struck. I wasn't capable at that point of working out the best method of receiving. I glanced at the front row of classmates' faces, all being focussed on me, or at least, on my hand. The boys were smirking and girls had looks of either horror or pity, I wasn't sure which. I felt a tap under my hand from the cane, signalling to me that I should raise it.

The swish as it descended seemed to drown any other sounds followed by a crack as it cut across my hand. For a few seconds I thought that my hand was about to leave my wrist, the experience of pain made me close my eyes and I sensed that there was at least a tear there, which I instantly knew must not be seen by my classmates. The antidote was to smile. I now knew why a smile appeared on the faces of the older and more experienced sufferers.

I looked away towards the door of the adjoining class-room. Through the glass panel I could see my sister, Joyce. She had seen the whole sorry episode. Surely she would show some pity for her loving older brother? Not likely. I could lip-read her remark: "I shall tell Mum when I get home that you have had the cane."

I realised instantly that would mean another telling off.

At least now the pain was subsiding and a numbness was taking over. I could not feel my thumb or fingers for hours after. I did not again make the mistake of losing concentration when the headmaster was taking our class.

As the war progressed, more aircraft arrived on the airfield. With the planes, came more air crew to fly them: first of all, Australian airmen from half-way around the world, and later the American Air Force, who brought Super Fortress planes, the largest aircraft we had seen so far at Fradley.

When more aircraft were required to replace those lost, to continue the attack on German towns and factories, bombers were sent from Fradley. It was inevitable that some of these would not return.

The villagers regularly heard the spluttering engines of damaged aircraft limping back to base after bombing raids, some of them having to make emergency landings owing to their undercarriages not functioning correctly.

Storage and loading of primed weapons was also a dangerous business. The sound of an exploding bomb would occasionally echo across the airfield. The contrasting silence immediately afterwards gave time to hope that no one had been killed.

To encourage saving, a bomb casing was placed in front of the village shop, onto which savings stamps could be stuck, after they had been purchased in the post office, which was within the shop. Messages were also written on the bomb in chalk, suggesting that this one was intended to kill Hitler. It obviously didn't leave Fradley at all, but I suppose it vented the frustration felt by some people and it certainly helped to finance the war, as the stamps could not be cashed once they had been stuck onto the bomb.

Savings stamps were intended to be bought as a way of saving money, blue ones having a value of one shilling (5p) and red ones, two shillings and sixpence (12½p). They were stuck into a savings book until a pound's worth had been saved, which could then be exchanged for a savings certificate.

Although these could be redeemed for cash at any time, most people didn't do so until after the war, when an interest on the money was also paid. The money saved meanwhile, helped with the war effort.

Towards the end of the war, after their nation had capitulated, Italian prisoners-of-war were used to do work on the land. They were brought to Fradley each day to clean out ditches alongside the roads. I remember being afraid when I saw them for the first time, in their dark brown uniforms with brightly-coloured patches sewn onto them in order that they could easily recognised by their guards, who stood at the end of the line with a rifle hanging from their shoulder.

Seeing the same children each day encouraged the Italians to talk to us and we were intrigued to listen to them attempting conversation in broken English.

Some of the prisoners were very good craftsmen and made rings from brass chunky threepenny pieces or out of pieces of Perspex, given to them by us children, which we had scavenged from crashed aircraft.

Little did I think at that time, as a young schoolboy, that within eight years, I would be a member of the British Army of Occupation in the north of their country.

Italian prisoners-of-war were also used to carry out labouring work within the secret underground ammunition store at RAF Fauld, just a few miles from Fradley.

The old gypsum mines in the village of Hanbury were used for storing thousands of tons of bombs, which were regularly transported to Fradley and other aerodromes to be loaded on to aircraft for use on bombing raids on Germany.

It is thought that although wooden spanners were provided to remove the detonators from bombs which were no longer required, in order to reduce the risk of sparks, one of the workers had used a metal spanner which caused a spark setting off a chain reaction of explosions.

At least two farms were blown up leaving an enormous crater and the local public house was badly damaged.

In all it was thought that about seventy people lost their lives, including farm workers, other civilians who happened to be in the area, three RAF personnel and six Italian prisoners of war.

The bodies of many people were never found. Numerous cows were also killed in the fields above the mines.

I was at school in Alrewas on that morning, 27 November 1944 when at eleven minutes past eleven the school building shook and desks rattled.

The headmaster walked quickly through each class room and told everyone to remain seated and to keep calm although he obviously didn't know the cause of the vibration.

I was used to hearing an occasional explosion having lived so near to Fradley aerodrome and thought that it had been made there but when I arrived home later in the day, my mother said that the sound of the explosion seemed to come from the opposite direction to the aerodrome.

Owing to the secrecy during the war years, it was at least a week before more accurate news reached Fradley even though Hanbury is only a few miles away.

The explosion at RAF Fauld was heard hundreds of miles away and was thought to be the largest World War Two explosion experienced in Britain and the world's greatest accidental explosion.

Chapter 8

THREE OR FOUR times each year the "Bug Nurse", as she was known by the children, visited the school. She wore navy blue dress with a starched white apron and a navy blue hat. The hat was never removed, maybe to ensure that none of the unwelcome visitors jumped from the children's hair onto hers. She always pulled our hair about very roughly whilst inspecting for nits.

My own hair was always kept short as was most boys' at that time, so there was very little chance of me catching anything which couldn't be easily seen. That didn't excuse me from having to go through the same ritual as my sister, however, of having regular washings by mother with coal tar soap, followed by a scraping of my scalp with a fine-toothed comb, which was supposed to show up the tell-tail signs of the dreaded lice as small white eggs. I always thought that they would be ideal for fishing, if it was possible to attach them to the hook.

The other unwelcome guest each year was the school dentist. When the call came for our class to line up outside and prepare for a dental inspection in the headmaster's office, a loud sigh went around the room.

The smell of the sterilizing solution was enough to make me feel ill before I even sat in the chair.

The same dentist and nurse came each year for the

whole of my school life. The nurse was a short, stocky blonde lady, about fifty years old and the dentist, who seemed as old as my grandfather, had hands that didn't stop shaking.

"Open wide," the nurse squealed, as "Shaker" thrust the mirror and probe into my mouth. He couldn't hold either of them still, which puzzled me as to how he could look at any individual tooth long enough to decide whether it required attention. After the instruments had rattled around my teeth for a few seconds, he said something in technical jargon to the nurse, which I hoped meant that they were all satisfactory.

No such luck. A few days later the official notifications were handed out to most of my class, by Miss Jones, my teacher, which had to be taken home to mother for her signature authorising the treatment. The kids who didn't have their names called out all cheered, knowing they hadn't got to suffer and would enjoy teasing those who had later that week.

During wartime neither toothbrushes nor toothpaste could be bought. My mother used to put some salt on a saucer and tell me to wet my finger, dip it in the salt and rub it around my teeth to clean them. I used to make believe that I had done it and tip the salt away without her knowing, as I didn't like the bitter taste of the salt.

I always talked Mum into making a note on the dental form that she had no objection to me having teeth extracted but did not want me to have any filled.

I had seen the drill, which was propelled by the dentist pushing a pedal up and down with his foot. I envisaged the old man not pedalling fast enough, resulting in the drill being embedded in my tooth or even worse in my gum, when he had one of his bad shakes.

The day arrived when my name was called in class to go for treatment. This was not carried out in the school, maybe in order that the other pupils didn't hear the screams.

A dental chair was set up in a room at the Odd Fellows Hall, a walk of about five hundred metres along the main street of the village. We were sent off in pairs, probably because it was more likely that a lone child would run off before reaching the hall. We sat in the main hall awaiting our turn, ears pricked, listening for any whimper from the poor kid being held down in the chair in the adjoining committee room.

Eventually it was my turn. I was instructed by the nurse to sit in the chair and to open my mouth wide. The dentist's hand suddenly appeared in front of my face holding a syringe with a needle on the end which looked to me as big as a pitch fork.

"He's surely not going to stick that into me," I thought.

"Open wider!" the nurse screeched grabbing my hands, but before I could react I felt a sharp pain in my gum which made tears fill my eyes. I was told to go back and sit in the main hall until I was called again. Slowly my jaw became numb. I thought I was becoming paralysed, however, I reassured myself that whatever the dentist did now, I would not be able to feel it. How wrong I was. I suspect that he had frozen the wrong part of my gum.

I lost three teeth that day, each one crumbling under the pressure of those ancient pincers. There was no one more pleased than me when I was told to get out of the chair and to wash my mouth out over the sink.

The walk back to school seemed quite enjoyable and I didn't even mind being teased about not being able to speak normally, owing to my lips being numb and uncontrollable. Even Miss Jones sympathised with me.

Although Mr. McKnight normally taught the senior pupils, he occasionally took over my class for special arithmetic lessons after we had reached our tenth birthday.

I hadn't realised why until Miss Jones, who was our

class teacher, informed us that we would be taking an examination shortly called 'the Scholarship', later to be called the Eleven-Plus.

Most of our class sat the examination over a few days in January 1945. I remember an arithmetic paper, which didn't prove to be too difficult after the concentrated effort made under the strict instruction of Mr. McKnight, an English paper, requiring a couple of essays to be written and a couple of multi-choice answer papers based on general knowledge.

I had forgotten all about even having taken the exam, when, one morning in April, after assembly prayers, the headmaster said that he had an announcement to make with regard to the results of the Scholarship examination.

"Two of you have been successful in passing the first part," he said. "Helen Barker and Colin Russell, please come out to the front."

I was too surprised to move. The boy standing next to me gave me a push to help me on my way, as the headmaster shouted, "Come on, Russell. You will have to move quicker than that if you go to Lichfield!" He congratulated us both and explained that the second part of the exam would be taken at the higher school in a few weeks' time.

"Now," he said to Helen, "You can go home and tell your parents about your success."

He faced me and continued, "You can't go all the way home to Fradley to tell your mother, as you'd be away all day!"

So I had to contain my excitement all day, before I could tell my mum. I wondered how she would take the news. If I went to the grammar school, it would mean extra expense which maybe she could not afford, with Dad still being abroad in the Army. Nevertheless I was thrilled as well as apprehensive at the thought of going to a grammar school. My friends immediately started to call me a

"Grammar Dog", which I didn't like, as I felt that it was going to separate me from them.

I sensed that when I broke the news to my mother, she had mixed feelings. She realised that if I went to the grammar school, it meant that I would have to cycle about five miles to Lichfield each day, and I didn't own a bike good enough to cope with the daily journey. There was a bike in the garage, however, belonging to Dad, which I was already using occasionally. As he was away from home, I couldn't see why I should not use it regularly.

However, I still had to pass the second part of the exam before definite decisions could be made.

It was generally thought that the war with Germany would not last much longer as the Russian troops were advancing on Berlin very quickly. The newspapers were full of maps showing the daily advances of both the Russians on the eastern front and the British and American forces from the west. Perhaps my dad would return home much quicker than I had envisaged.

An armistice was signed by the allies and the enemy and peace was declared.

We arrived at school on 8th May 1945, to be told by the headmaster that the day was to be called "VE Day" and we would have a day's holiday. Everyone cheered at the announcement of an of an extra day's holiday.

We ran back to Fradley to tell our mothers the good news. Anyone who had a flag of any kind hung it out of the bedroom window. Several of our mums met to have a cup of tea together, maybe to discuss the future.

They were obviously delighted that their husbands were now in less danger, except of course for those still involved in the Far Eastern war with the Japanese. At least one young man from Fradley, Tom Green, was known to be a prisoner-of-war in Japanese hands.

There were no real celebrations in the village until a

few months after, when most fathers were back home. A sports afternoon was held in the field at the rear of the school, when small prizes were given to the winners and tea and sandwiches served.

The first time that ice cream was on sale at the shop, the news quickly spread amongst my friends. Well, we always got the inside information first, having our friend John, living on the premises. We all scrounged a few coppers from our mothers to buy a cone and a cylindrical shaped piece of vanilla ice cream, which tasted wonderful after having waited so long to enjoy the experience once again.

We removed sticky papers from the ice cream and stuck them all over the head of Fordy's old horse, who was standing between the shafts of a cart in the roadway. The poor horse used to stand there most of the day, as Mr. Ford was a sandwich short of a picnic and unfortunately was teased a bit by us boys.

The bells on churches could now be rung at any time. As it was my duty to pump the organ for morning services, I was asked to arrive at church half an hour earlier to ring the lone bell before the service.

It had not been rung since the war started, almost six years before, so after the initial rings there was a clatter on the tiled roof made by the deposits left on the bell, by the birds over the last few years.

Most Sunday mornings, Mrs. Lakin, who lived near to the church, was brought in her wheelchair by one of the congregation. I was usually asked to help lift her in the chair up the two steps at the church entrance. After the service I was sometimes asked to push her, in the chair, to her friend's house at Alrewas and ran back home in time for the best meal of the week, Mum's Sunday dinner.

My mother was notified by letter of the date when I had to attend the grammar school for an interview and final exam. She went with me on the Midland Red bus and we walked up Saint John Street to the school entrance. I think she was more scared than me, when she saw the masters dressed in black gowns and boys all wearing school uniform, something neither of us had been used to at the schools we had attended.

We were ushered into the school secretary's office and asked to take a seat. There were two other boys waiting, one with his mother and one alone.

Eventually it was my turn to be called in to see the head master. Mr. Marlar sat behind a big desk in his office and beckoned to me to sit down in front of him. He asked me a few questions about my present school and about the village where I lived, followed by what my father did for a living. When I informed him that Dad was still in the Army, he asked me what I knew about his regiment and where he was stationed at the time. Then the serious questions were fired at me.

A couple of mental arithmetic problems and few questions on history. I was quite surprised at his next question "How far can a rabbit run into a wood?"

"Not far", I thought, if one of the Fradley farmers was behind it with his gun! I hadn't got a clue really, but started to mumble something. He quickly put me out of my misery – like the rabbit – and explained that he could only run halfway in, as he would then be running out. I have never forgotten that humiliation.

With the interview over, much quicker than I had expected, Mum and I walked into the town and did a bit of shopping before we caught the bus home.

It was about at this time when I first witnessed a death in my family. My grandmother, who came just occasionally to our house, was a very strict Victorian lady. My sister and I dreaded her coming to stay. If she was in the house, the rules changed. Even my dad voluntarily avoided doing things which might upset her.

We often played a game of cards on Sunday with him, but not if Grandma was around. She regularly told me to use my backbone to sit upright and not to lean on the back of a chair.

She was taken ill whilst staying with some friends. The message was sent via the postman to my mother and I was given a note by my mum to deliver, on my bike, to Mrs. Haskew, asking her to arrange for my Grandmother to be brought to our house.

She was made comfortable in a bed in the front room. "At least, in there," I explained to my sister, " She can't see what we are doing in the living room."

Dad was still away in the Army, so he didn't see any of the comings and goings of aunts and uncles, each staying a night to keep watch over her. The sound of her continual coughing echoed around the house. After a couple of weeks, the poor lady died from pneumonia and her funeral was held at Fradley church.

Her coffin was brought in and taken out through the front door. That door was only ever opened, as far as I remember, for the doctor to enter or for coffins to be taken out. Everyone else used the back door. Even if a stranger knocked the front door, Mum would walk round to the front from the back to speak to them.

King Edward VI Grammar School, Lichfield 1945 - 1950

Chapter 9

THE OFFICIAL letter arrived, notifying my mother that I had been selected to go to King Edward VI Grammar School. Although apprehensive, I was excited at the thought of having the opportunity of taking subjects which were not on the curriculum at Alrewas School. I would also be able to wear long trousers.

Mum must have been concerned about the cost of additional clothes and equipment required, all due to the

Fig 17: King Edward VI Grammar School, Lichfield

fact that I'd had a lucky examination day. My friend, John Hardy, had already attended King Edward's for a couple of years, having passed a Thirteen-Plus examination, so it was very nice to go to my new school with someone who had already the experience of a first day there.

I used my dad's bike, as although the Second World War had officially ended, he was still stationed in Belgium. My mother had been told, that as clothing coupons were still required to purchase clothes, it would not be compulsory to wear school uniform until I had outgrown my present clothing. I had talked Mum into buying me some long trousers, however, so I did feel a little more grown up. Until now, like most boys under the age of eleven, I had worn short grey pants and grey stockings, held up with garters just below the knee. I continually complained about the garters cutting into my legs and talked my mum into allowing me to tie a piece of tape around each stocking, which I considered more manly than wearing garters, like the girls.

Within a few months, my jacket was becoming too small so with the help of my earnings from my newspaper round, I was allowed to have a blazer with the school badge upon it, together with a school cap, the wearing of which became compulsory to and from school and at any other time outside school when uniform was being worn.

Rugby was played on games days during the autumn and winter terms with a few weeks of cross-country running included, so it was essential to have the kit and boots, which could be bought from the second-hand stall at the school.

John showed me where to find the notice board, which was covered with information, showing that I was to be in form 3B, a member of Garrick House and was allocated a numbered parking stand in the bike shed and also a numbered hat and coat hook in the cloak room.

A bell was rung at start and finish of school and also at change of lessons. I had to quickly get used to the layout of the school, as the class moved around to different rooms dependent upon the lesson being taken, quite different from my previous school, where we remained in the same room all day. Assembly was held in the hall each morning before the start of lessons, where the headmaster, after a hymn was sung and prayers said, read out any items of interest, such as results of any sporting competitions in which a school team had been involved.

Being an all-boys' school, the teachers were mainly men, but as it was still being run on a wartime basis, there were two lady teachers, Ma Fletcher, an old spinster, who taught geography and Miss Jones, a younger lady, who took Latin.

I always wondered how knowing Latin would help me, as I didn't know of any country who spoke the lingo. Ma Fletcher usually at some time during the lesson would sit on the front of her desk, showing about a couple of inches of dusky pink bloomers, pinched in with tight elastic and a wide garter an inch or so above her knee holding up her thick stockings. Unfortunately, the young Miss Jones never did anything so revealing. She would, however, often give one of us a clip round the ear because we had forgotten how to recite the verb *amo, amas, amat, amamus, amatis, amant...*

There were several subjects taught, which were quite new to me, Latin and French being the most difficult, physics and chemistry the most interesting and woodwork and art the most relaxing The standard was obviously higher and a written report was produced at the end of each term, showing not only the percentage marks for each subject but also comments by each subject teacher, form teacher and the headmaster. Fortunately, after the first year, "B" forms didn't continue to take Latin, which was a great relief to me.

Like my old headmaster at Alrewas School, the majority of masters smoked pipes, so there were always differing flavours of tobacco to be smelled around the buildings. They were generally too old or unfit to be called up into the forces. Most of the time, during school hours, they wore black gowns and like the boys, they called the headmaster "Sir".

During my second year at King Edward's several new masters, who had by now completed war service, arrived at the school. The headmaster Mr. Marlar, retired and was replaced by a much younger man, Mr. Bill Richards. His aim, certainly at first, was to shake up the whole school, pupils and teachers alike, to leave no doubt in anyone's mind as to who was boss. He scared the life out of my form one day, when he heard a lot of noise coming from our room as we awaited a teacher coming to take the next lesson. The door burst open as he roared at us to be quiet. Fortunately he was not carrying his cane, otherwise I am sure we would all have received six strokes.

Physical training and games were taken over by younger, fitter men. Mr. Joe Murray, who had been a PTI in the forces, joined the staff and took each class for PT. He made us work hard in the gymnasium. There was no more hiding behind the vaulting box, as some of us managed to do whilst old Harry Peach was in charge. He used a clever way of embarrassment, which seemed to give us the courage to try any difficult apparatus. He taught me to swim, which I never learned to do in the canal, even though I spent a lot of the summer holidays in it with my friend Gel.

Mr. Peach was given the job of taking religious instruction, before being put out to grass himself. Mr. Lionel Brockwell took charge of the rugby teams. Being a regular player with Lichfield Rugby Club, his coaching changed the school teams dramatically into squads who rarely lost.

School dinners, served in the small school dining room, were limited to just a select few. The alternative was to take sandwiches or go to the civic café, alongside the Methodist Church in the town. As my friend John had decided on the latter, I decided to join him. Those of us with bikes at school, we were able to ride down there at lunch time, but those who came by bus or train had to walk. Although I liked vegetables, I wasn't too keen on a pile of green cabbage every day, so after a few weeks, I decided to take sandwiches. I was also available then to join the other members of my form playing football at lunch time.

Rugby was a new game for me. As soon as I had learned the rules, and as I was a big kid, I was selected to play for the junior house team and eventually for the school colts team. The school teams played against other grammar schools within an area of about twenty miles, some of these matches being played on Saturday afternoons. After the game, I was able to have a shower at school, an experience I had not had before. If I could prove to Mum that I had already showered, she would let me off going through the ordeal of a bath and having to clean it afterwards.

Having homework to do after getting home from school curtailed some of my other activities. I didn't have time to deliver newspapers before school but continued to do it on Saturday mornings. Most evenings towards the end of the week, I delivered groceries from the shop to the outlying houses. It was still important to earn what I could to help Mum as much as possible.

I took up another hobby, now that I was older, that of taking train numbers. I usually went "train-spotting" with my friend John. We managed to get a book each showing the different classes of steam engines, with a list of their names and numbers. Those with names were the ones we were most interested in seeing and Trent Valley station was the ideal place to see them. A record was kept by each of us of the engines we saw by underlining the names in our books. We were particularly excited if we saw a "streek", a streamlined engine. In fact we had a serious telling-off by the station master one day for running across the line to get on to the platform, when we saw a streamlined engine on the inside local line, obviously going to stop.

One late afternoon, a few months after the war had ended, a troop train loaded with American servicemen pulled into the station whilst a faster through train went by. They spotted John and myself sitting on the embankment and started to throw, first of all a few packets of chewing gum and then, coins to us. They were all cheering merrily, obviously returning home to the USA and were no longer in need of British currency. We collected up the pennies around us and headed for home, hoping that we still had a some coupons left, now that we had the money to buy a few sweets.

The American airmen were missed in the Fradley public houses. They had spent a lot of their money in the Bull's Head and the Bell Inn. Both pubs were situated on the main road, the Bull's Head almost opposite Fradley Lane and the Bell adjacent to the canal bridge. I enjoyed talking to the "Yanks", especially when they handed out some chewing gum or chocolate. Most boys collected used cigarette packets and match boxes discarded by the Americans. Lucky Strike and Camel were the most common fag packets. There was also an enormous amount of "garbage", to use their word, deposited at the marl pits tip, which was situated at the junction of the main road and Fox Lane.

I often roamed all over it scavenging for anything which could be reused. It was mainly used for depositing ashes from the coal fires in the houses, but there were often half-used batteries dumped by the Yanks. With a length of cable and a few bulbs borrowed from our bicycle lamps, I could make up a lighting display in the shed. The practice certainly taught me the basics of electricity, positive and negative terminals, and wiring in series or parallel.

Even after peace in Europe had been declared, aeroplanes still circled Fradley. Many new models arrived and accidents still occurred. Late one afternoon, I witnessed an horrific crash, when a Mosquito, a model quite new to Fradley, appeared to be carrying out aerobatics, when it went out of control and nose-dived into a field along Hay End, fortunately well away from any houses.

With my friend John, I raced on my bike towards the tell-tail plume of smoke, only to see in the distance, a big hole where the plane had disintegrated as it plunged into the ground. We were stopped quickly in our tracks at the sight of smouldering human flesh in the road before us and the first RAF personnel on the scene shouting at us to "Clear off!"

When Dad was demobbed, although pleased to see him, I at first resented the fact that I was no longer "the man of the house". He made decisions with regard to the garden, when to start digging, where the potatoes would be planted and when the beans needed to be "sticked".

I also had to stop wearing his shoes and riding his bike. He realised that my old bike, a combination of scrap parts and without brakes, was not suitable for travelling to Lichfield each day, so he bought me a new one.

I had seen a BSA bike in Jones's window, on the corner of Bore Street and Bird Street in Lichfield. When I told him that it was priced at thirteen pounds, I thought that would be the last I would hear of it, but on the following Saturday morning, I accompanied him on the crossbar of his bike into Lichfield, he agreed to buy it and I rode it home. I think he must have used the small lump sum each member of the forces was given when they were demobbed.

A WARTIME SCHOOLBOY: MEMORIES OF FRADLEY

Professional football clubs started to reorganise the football leagues again, to start in the spring of 1946. Some of the professionals from before the war had missed the opportunity to play in the league for six years, having to be satisfied with playing occasionally for the branch of services to which they belonged.

My father and grandfather were both supporters of Aston Villa, so it was inevitable, I suppose, that I should also become a Villa supporter. In fact, during my very early years, I didn't even know that any other team existed.

To get to Villa Park from Fradley proved to be quite an ordeal. For the first few home matches of the new season, Dad arranged to go with a group of colleagues in a hired taxi from Alrewas. I was desperate to go with them but afraid of the car journey, owing to suffering from travel sickness whenever I had been any distance of more than five miles by car or bus. The temptation of seeing my favourite team, however, was enough for me to risk going in the car to the second home match of the season, but before we arrived at our destination, the driver, Mr. Alf Wood, had to stop to allow me to be sick on the roadside. To add to my disappointment Villa lost by two goals to nil.

After that episode, I don't think Dad could stand the embarrassment, so whenever I went with him, we travelled by bus from Fradley to Lichfield and then by train to Witton station via Walsall, about a four-hour journey each way.

The bike ride to and from school each day became very monotonous after the first year or two. The prevailing west wind, directly against me when riding towards Lichfield, proved to be a problem on days when it was pouring with rain. I was often soaked when I arrived at school and had to dry out by sitting on the heating pipes in the cloakroom. The journey was an even bigger problem during the winters. On frosty mornings, I often lost control of my bike and finished up lying on the roadway. For some reason, which I never managed to understand, my friend Gel's sister Marion, who used to accompany us most mornings on her way to work in Lichfield, never tumbled off at all.

Often the snow was too deep to ride a bike easily and as the earliest Midland Red bus didn't pass the end of Fradley Lane until 10.45am., the only way to get to school was to walk and hope that sometimes a vehicle would stop to give me a lift.

During the winter of 1947 however, the snow was so deep that very few vehicles ventured along the road, so most days I walked to and from school, a distance of five miles each way. It was often around ten o'clock when I arrived, in time for morning break, when I could thaw a bottle of frozen milk over a radiator to get a drink. It would be dark when I arrived home with my balaclava hat frozen on to my face. The walk proved to be more exciting than the bike ride, especially when the lanes into Fradley village were impassable owing to deep snow drifts. To bypass the drifts, it was often easier to walk on top of the hedge.

Towards the end of each school year at King Edward's we sat an exam in each subject, the aim being to take the School Certificate in the fifth year. A report was sent to my parents at the end of each term, showing my marks in each subject for term work and examinations, with a few lines of comment by each teacher.

My work in mathematics and science subjects was usually quite good but I struggled to reach the required standard in English literature and history. It was essential that at least a pass mark was obtained in English language in the School Certificate Examination, otherwise you were not presented with a certificate at all, even if all your other subjects were passed satisfactorily.

The amount of homework increased as I got older, so I found that in the latter years at school, I had very little spare time after I had completed the few jobs that I carried out at the shop on Saturday mornings.

At the age of fourteen I played for the school colts rugby team and the following year I was a regular player for the 1st. XV, so my time was fully taken with either study or sport. In my first game played for the 1st's, at home versus Burton Grammar School, I scored a try. That must have impressed the sports master, as I was selected to play in every match during the season. We played against other grammar schools across Staffordshire and Warwickshire, both at home and away. After the match, there was always a very nice tea of jam sandwiches and cake, provided for all the players.

The match that most of us looked forward to and wanted to play in, was the annual game against the Old Boys' team, which was usually made up from ex-King Edward's boys who played for Lichfield Rugby Club. In my final

Fig 18: King Edward VI School Colts Rugby team, 1948-49. Back row: Weaver, Richards, Selley, Horobin, Birks, Clements, Bowler, Owen (linesman); Seated: Russell, Clift, Heath, Shaw, Langley, Fullelove, McCabe; Front, Price, Watson.

Fig 19: King Edward VI School, 1st XV Rugby team, 1949-50.
Back row: Mr. J. Murray, Fullelove, Linford, Russell, Pulley, Derry,
Langley, Mr. L. Brockwell, Ferguson; Seated: Herbert, Dent, Simmons,
Stevens (Capt.), Smith, Preston, Fairgrieves; Front: Heath, Bradford

year, our school team won the match, so for at least a week we were treated like gods not only by the other pupils but also by the teachers.

There was also a Cadet Force run on Thursday afternoons by a few of the masters. Lower fifth formers were allowed to join the Army section, and were given a uniform, to be worn only on parade days. There was a choice of transferring to the Air Force section after the first year but I decided to remain with the Army section and learned drill and the basics of the weapons, which I found beneficial when doing my National Service in the Army.

Discipline was strictly enforced at King Edward's. In addition to punishment dealt out by the masters, prefects appointed by the headmaster from the upper sixth form were also allowed to give detentions and punishment to any student breaking school rules.

Along with several of my colleagues, at the age of fifteen,

Fig 20: Myself with my friend Gel,
taken in 1949 at Arkwright Town

I was given six strokes of the slipper across my behind for entering a room during lunch time, which was out of bounds.

During my summer holiday in 1949, one of Dad's sisters invited me to go and stay at her house for a week. My aunt lived at Arkwright Town, a village near to Chesterfield, in Derbyshire. I don't know why it was called a town, as it only had one shop and a post office. However, the holiday was so good that the week was extended to about three weeks. My three cousins, who lived there, were girls and all older than me, so although they did not fancy a game of football, I managed to get a game most days with some of the local boys.

The teams in the football league had started their pre-season practice matches, so my uncle, who enjoyed watching football, took me, twice each week to watch games at either Chesterfield, Sheffield and Derby. I was fortunate to enjoy the good times with my uncle that would have been lavished on his own son if there had been one. So there was no complaint from me about there being only girl cousins.

They took me along with them to the theatre on Saturday evenings to see a variety show or to the fairground, to have a ride on the dodgems. I think the local older boys used to speak to me as an excuse to get the opportunity to chat up my cousins. I don't think they would have even looked at me otherwise.

After that holiday, I often went to stay for a weekend and took a friend with me.

I sat my School Certificate Examination in May 1950, knowing that I would be leaving King Edward's in July to start work. I knew that my parents could not afford to keep me at school any longer. It was essential that I obtained a certificate, otherwise my dream of wanting to become an architect would be drastically reduced to a life, still in the building industry, as a bricklayer like that of my father and my grandfather.

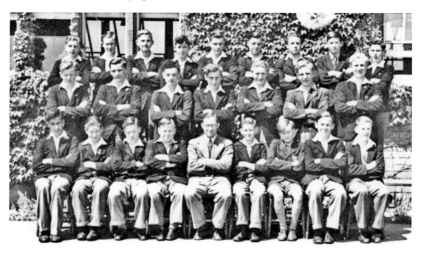

Fig 21: Me, age 15 (third from the right in the middle row) and my classmates in the "Remove" form at King Edward's. This class was between the Lower Fifth and Fifth forms.

I was fortunate that I did pass in English language and at least five other subjects to be awarded with a certificate and was successful in getting a job immediately, not with an architectural practice, however, but to assist in the Quantity Surveyors' office at J. R. Deacon Ltd., the largest building contractors in Lichfield.

So I bade farewell to school and started to work for a living, but that is another story.

Index

INDEX

Myself, February 2020

About the Author

AFTER LEAVING school I spent eighteen months working in the Quantity Surveyors' office of J R Deacon Ltd, a large building contractor in Lichfield, awaiting my call-up into the forces at eighteen years old to serve two years' National Service.

I chose the Army as I had been a member of the Army Cadet Force during my final two years at school and after initial training with the North Staffordshire Regiment at Whittington Barracks near Lichfield, I spent the remainder of my two years' service in Northern Italy with the 1st. Battalion as part of The British Element Trieste Force on the Yugoslav border. Quite a contrast from my life in Fradley Village. I was fortunate whilst there to play rugby for both the Battalion and 24th. Infantry Brigade teams.

After being demobilized, on of all days, April Fools' Day 1954, I walked home knowing that I would again be able to enjoy my mother's lovely dinners and to sleep in my own little bedroom.

I was retained on reserve in the Territorial Army for five years although this was cancelled after three years, when it was decided that National Service was no longer to be continued.

I decided to change my sport from rugby to play football for Fradley F. C. when the club was formed in 1954. What a lovely change to be playing again with my friends in the field where we played together as youngsters but were now representing our village.

I returned to my job at J. R. Deacon Ltd. where I met Lydia, who eventually became my wife, but I had to complete five years of evening classes at college to obtain my qualification to become a surveyor before we were married in 1959. We were fortunate to have two children, Peter and Theresa, and eventually, two granddaughters, Kerri and Hannah.

I worked for two other contractors before having the satisfaction of being self-employed for the final thirty-five years of my working life.

Although we have moved house four times, Lydia and I have always lived within ten miles of my childhood home of Fradley and now, in retirement, live a mile away in Alrewas where I also spent three years at the village school.

My original memories of my school life, from which this book has been taken, were written fifteen years ago and were intended to be a record for my children and grandchildren to read how I remember my school life during wartime.

Colin Russell
Alrewas
2020

Follow-up reading

Colin Russell mentions the explosion at RAF Fauld, the massive underground ammunition dump a few miles from Fradley, on 27 November 1944. You can read more about this in the expertly-researched ***Voices from the Explosion: RAF Fauld, the World's Largest Accidental Blast, 1944*** by Valerie Hardy. The author was a child at the time of the disaster and lived at Fauld House Farm, close to the site. She was thus in an ideal position to return in later years to record the testimonies of those who had experienced the explosion, before those memories were lost for ever. The print book was originally published in 2015 by Dark River, Bennion Kearny Ltd, and a new 75th anniversary edition by Woldscot is now available. It is also on Amazon.co.uk as a Kindle ebook (ASIN: B017YZQTR6).

For detailed information about the life of a Wellington bomber pilot, like those trained at Fradley, we recommend the fascinating ***They Also Served – An Autobiography of a Wellington Bomber Pilot*** by Les Hather. Written in his retirement, using his diaries, his flying log books, and wartime operational records in the Public Record Office, it was originally privately published in 1997. Thanks to his son, it is now available on Amazon.co.uk as a Kindle ebook (ASIN: B0093N7UIA).

The Day the Dump Went Up & The Flying Kangaroos: Two Stories of Wartime Burton (RAF Fauld and RAF Lichfield) by local journalist Mark Rowe, is also very interesting follow-up reading. The book was first self-published in 1999, and in a different format in 2004. The author has also written ***After the Dump Went Up: The Untold Story.*** Second-hand copies of both books are on sale via online dealers.

A.L.P.

A SELECTION OF BOOKS PUBLISHED BY LÉONIE PRESS

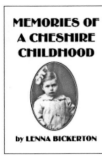

NOW AN e-BOOK

MEMORIES OF A CHESHIRE CHILDHOOD

by LENNA BICKERTON

For more details
and postage costs
contact
Léonie Press:
13 Vale Road
Hartford, Northwich
CW8 1PL
Tel: 01606 75660
www.leoniepress.com
jack@leoniepress.com

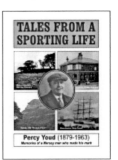

TALES FROM A SPORTING LIFE

Percy Youd (1879-1963)
Memories of a Mersey man who made his mark

MEMORIES OF A CHESHIRE CHILDHOOD
LENNA BICKERTON

Lenna Bickerton spent her early years during the First World War living with her grandparents in the close-knit community of Lostock Gralam. Her mother, a young war widow, worked in an ammunition factory at Wincham and afterwards in domestic service in Manchester, travelling home on the Sunday afternoon "dripping train" to see her daughter.

When Lenna's mother married again, the small family eventually moved into one of the first council houses to be built at Rudheath – a piece of good fortune they regarded as little short of a miracle. Lenna lived on the same estate until she died in Nov 1999.

In her book Lenna describes life in those far-off days through the sharp senses of a child. Her memories are vivid: duck eggs for breakfast, dancing to Grandad's gramophone, a near-tragedy at Hesketh's watermill, her schooldays, the sights and sounds of old Northwich, the smells of wild flowers, busy boat traffic on the Trent and Mersey Canal – and the menacing 'Ginny Greenteeth'.

The young Lenna roamed the fields, woods and flashes around Lostock Gralam and Rudheath in a carefree way any modern child would envy. She said: "Boredom was a word we never used in our childhood. Our imagination came into play to make up for the lack of material things and, most of all, we had freedom to wander at will in the countryside."

This is a special memorial edition of one of the Léonie Press's most popular and highly praised books. It contains a photograph of Lenna and an obituary report.

ISBN 978-1-901253-13-9 94pp, 11 b+w photos, A5 format,
Price: £4.99
e-Book Kindle format ISBN: 978-1-909727-04-5
Amazon No: (ASIN) B00H2YWN5W. Price £1.99

TALES FROM A SPORTING LIFE
Memories of a Mersey man who made his mark
PERCY YOUD (1879-1963)

When Percy Youd was born in Frodsham in 1879, the Manchester Ship Canal was soon to be constructed nearby. From an early age, natural ability and a marksman's eye singled him out as an outstanding shot with anything from a muzzle-loader to a 12-bore shotgun. His quarry included game in the Cheshire hills and wildfowl on the Mersey estuary. He was a fearless fist-fighter and an excellent athlete, setting a record for the gruelling Helsby Hill race (he trained on sherry) – among many other sporting achievements.

Percy's first job in 1893 was at the Helsby cable works and in 1902 he moved to its sister factory at Prescot as a foreman. A few years later the company asked him to take on the Imperial Hotel on the edge of the 'Wire Works' complex. He later moved to Birkenhead. He was a keen member of the Conservative Club in Ellesmere Port and set up iin the town as an auctioneer. He led many shooting parties and his marksmanship was the subject of betting.

He organised a 100,000-name petition to try to save his Chinese friend, convicted murderer Lock Ah Tam, from the gallows and claimed friendship with Selwyn Lloyd who was MP for the Wirral.

In old age Percy wrote some of his memories down in a 22,000-word unpunctuated "lump" of vividly descriptive prose which was discovered after his death – including the script of the Frodsham 'soul-caking' play. This book contains the gently edited text, together with family portraits, old photographs and postcards, press cuttings and background information. There is also an account by his daughter of her childhood with him in the 1920s after he abducted her from his estranged wife.

ISBN 978-1-901253-31-3, 188pp, A5
format, 94 illustrations. Price £8.99.

A SELECTION OF BOOKS PUBLISHED BY LÉONIE PRESS

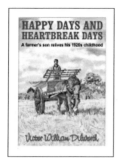

NOW AN e-BOOK

For more details
and postage costs
contact
Léonie Press:
13 Vale Road
Hartford, Northwich
CW8 1PL
Tel: 01606 75660
www.leoniepress.com
jack@leoniepress.com

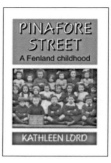

HAPPY DAYS AND HEARTBREAK DAYS
A farmer's son relives
his 1920s childhood
VICTOR DILWORTH

After Victor Dilworth drove by chance through the village where he was born in the 1920s, he started to recall his earliest memories of life on the family farm, Hinstock Grange. In his retirement, as he concentrated on these recollections, they became so real that it felt as though he had been reborn into those times and was actually reliving his experiences.

Describing long-gone sights, sounds, smells and emotions, he employs a turn of phrase so evocative and exact that reading this book is like watching a vivid video being played in the mind, 'filmed' through the eyes of a toddler and small boy. The scenes are set in his native Shropshire and also in Cheshire. The youngest of the family ('the scratching of the pot'), Victor finds that his hard-working parents have little time for him until he can do some useful work. Affection comes from his big sister, his grandfather and his beloved dog, Rover. Always anxious to learn, he watches the family milking cows, making prize-winning cheese and tending the many animals. He sees lambs being born and under threat of a whack from the cow strap he refrains from touching the baby chicks as they emerge from their shells in the incubator. He helps the farm waggoner to oil the horse-drawn mowing machine and accompanies his father to feed the sheep, on a float pulled by Dolly the pony. He learns about the cycle of life and death on the farm and comes to realise "that all creatures on earth are dependent on each other, just like the strands of a spider's web suspended on a hedgerow in the autumn."

ISBN 978-1-901253-34-4 108pp, A5, colour &
b+w photographs   Price £6.99
e-book Kindle format ISBN 987-1-909727-10-6
Amazon No: (ASIN) B00LAQ5LJI, Price £2.47

PINAFORE STREET
A Fenland Childhood
KATHLEEN LORD

Kathleen Lord (née Hall) was born in 1914 and spent most of her childhood in Boston, Lincolnshire. Her father worked in the building trade and the family moved to a claustrophobically small two-up, two-down cottage in Freiston Road when she was four. It had a shared cold water tap in the front garden of the house next door and a two-seater privy, complete with fly-papers, at the bottom of the garden. This was Kathleen's refuge when she wanted to read her comics in peace and the embarrassing setting for her mother's mortifying encounter with the 'dillyman'.

In vivid detail, this charming book describes everyday life in the town and surrounding fens seen through the eyes of a young girl. The story covers the aftermath of the First World War and the 1920s, and brings a long-gone era sharply back into focus.

Kathleen writes about the neighbours, children's games, fights with her little sister, her soft-hearted father's reluctant tellings-off, visits to The Pictures for tuppence, excursions to the local drains and rivers, trips "Down Below", schooldays (complete with liberty bodices, serge frocks and pinafores for the girls), the thrills of Empire Day, Sunday School treats and the Fair, learning to swim in the gender-segregated Corporation baths and wobbling her way to cycling prowess.

She describes junior meetings of the Sons of Temperance, her time in the Girl Guides, digging and delving on her father's allotment, the visiting anglers from Sheffield, Christmas rituals, and a stay with relations in Manchester when her father could find no work in Boston. When she was 19, Kathleen moved to Stamford, where she met her husband.

ISBN 978-1-901253-39-9 A5 paperback, 134pp,
b+w illust/photos Price £6.99